.99

BABYLON
AND THE OLD TESTAMENT

STUDIES IN BIBLICAL ARCHAEOLOGY NO. 8

BABYLON
AND THE
OLD TESTAMENT

ANDRÉ PARROT

Curator-in-Chief of the French National Museums,
Professor at the École du Louvre, Paris,
Director of the Mari Archaeological Expedition

PHILOSOPHICAL LIBRARY
NEW YORK

Translated by B. E. Hooke
from the French
BABYLONE ET L'ANCIEN TESTAMENT
(Delachaux et Niestlé, Neuchâtel, 1956)

*Published 1958, by the Philosophical Library, Inc.,
15 East 40th Street, New York, 16, N.Y.*

*Printed in Great Britain for Philosophical Library, Inc., by
The Bowering Press, Plymouth*

CONTENTS

Contents

[6]

LIST OF ILLUSTRATIONS

Plates 1 and 4 are reproduced from E. Unger's *Babylon*, by kind permission of the author.

[7]

Illustrations

[8]

Illustrations

[9]

Illustrations

[10]

Illustrations

[11]

Illustrations

(Figures taken from the author's *Ziggurats et Tour de Babel* and *Archéologie mésopotamienne* are reproduced by permission of the publishers, Messrs. Albin Michel. The other figures are based on original unpublished drawings by Pierre Hamelin.)

FOREWORD

I visited Babylon for the first time in 1930 and for the last time twenty years later, in 1950, and between these dates I revisited it on several occasions. The impression it always made on me was one of utter desolation.

The town is only a short distance from Baghdad, and a stream of tourists pours into it almost daily. They are generally deeply disappointed and almost with one voice exclaim that there is nothing to see. They expect to find palaces, temples, and the 'Tower of Babel'; they are shown only masses of ruins, most of them consisting of baked brick—that is to say, sun-dried clay blocks, grey-coloured and crumbling, and in no way impressive. The destruction wrought by man has been completed by the ravages of nature which still takes its toll of everything which excavation has brought to light. Eroded or undermined by rain, wind, and frost, the most magnificent monument, if it is not kept in repair, will return to the dust from which it was reclaimed. All that Koldewey patiently unearthed is thus doomed to disappear again. The site of his excavations, forty years afterwards, presents a heart-breaking spectacle—except for the area of the Ishtar gate. No human power can arrest this ceaseless spoliation. It is no longer possible to reconstruct Babylon; her destiny is accomplished. But it is possible to trace the successive stages of her history thanks to the excavations of archaeologists, and thanks also to the written documents which bring to life again the great figures of the past.

Among these documents the Old Testament writings are the most important, because Babylon came into collision with Jerusalem. But Jerusalem has managed to survive all its defeats and the repeated devastations which, when they occurred, seemed to be final. Babylon, on the other hand, has completely disappeared. Such has been the fate of all the great Mesopotamian capitals which have reverted to desert after having blazed like beacons through the centuries.

But on Mount Sion, the 'city of the great king' is watched over to-day by the threefold sign of the star, the cross, and the crescent, emblems of the one God. In the plain of Shinar, Marduk, god of the city and the State, has lost his worshippers. His son Nabu, the fixer of destinies, could not save his adherents from the fate which overtook the statue with the feet of clay. Shattered into fragments by the mysterious stone, the huge effigy, the very sight of which inspired terror, has been doomed to destruction. 'Like the chaff of the summer threshing-floors, the wind has scattered it.'

I

THE EXPLORATION
OF BABYLON

Babylon is situated on the River Euphrates in central Mesopotamia some fifty miles south of Baghdad, the capital of Iraq, and about four miles north of the small modern town of Hilleh, which has been built very largely of bricks salvaged from ancient monuments. The city stood in the centre of a magnificent plantation of palms and was provided with a permanent water supply. Moreover it enjoyed an exceptionally favourable situation on the trade route and main highway from the Persian Gulf to the Mediterranean. It is not surprising, in view of these almost ideal economic conditions, that its destiny should have been, as it were, taken for granted. On an old map of the world incised on a clay tablet now in the British Museum (fig. I) Babylon quite naturally is placed at the centre of the universe.[1]

The earliest reference to Babylon occurs in a text of King Shargalisharri of the Accadian dynasty (about 2350 B.C.) in the Sumerian form Ka-dingir (gate of god), which the Accadians translated literally

[1] A. Jeremias, *Handbuch der altorientalischen Geisteskultur*, figs. 89 and 90; E. Unger, *Babylon*, figs. 3 and 4. British Museum, Tablet No. 92687.

I. Babylon at the centre of the cosmos (from Unger, Babylon, *Pl. 3, fig. 4)*

as Bâb-ilu, with the same meaning. In later texts, dating from the Neo-Babylonian period (seventh–fourth centuries b.c.), the word Bâb-ilâni (gate of the gods) occurs, rendered by the Greeks $\beta\alpha\beta\upsilon\lambda\omega\nu$. From other documents, both cuneiform and biblical, it appears that Babylon was known by other names also,[1] among them Tintir^{ki} (wood of life) and E^{ki} (city of the canal?).

Unlike Nineveh, concerning which ancient writers had declared that no trace of the city remained, and the place where it had stood was unknown, Babylon, in spite of the destruction it suffered and the complete devastation of its site, was not completely obliterated. Traces of it remained in the form of a series of mounds (fig. II) known by the following names (from north to south): Bâbil (or Mujelibe), Kasr, Merkes, Homera, Ishin-Aswad, Amrân-ibn-Ali; a hollow or depression was known as Sakhn. It is clear that the ancient name has been preserved in the term Bâbil. We shall see later which ancient monuments are denoted by these Arabic terms. Other mounds are situated in the modern villages of Anana, Sinjar, Kweiresh and Jumjumma along the right and left banks of the river Euphrates.

It is not possible here to mention all the travellers who, from the time of Herodotus of Halicarnassus (fifth century B.C.) made the journey to Babylon.[2] If we confine ourselves to our own times, the first pilgrim was Rabbi Benjamin of Tudela (twelfth century) who seems to have been more interested in the number of Jews living near the city and in their synagogues than in the monuments of the past,

[1] E. Unger, 'Babylon' in *RLA*, p. 333.
[2] *History*, I, 178–88.

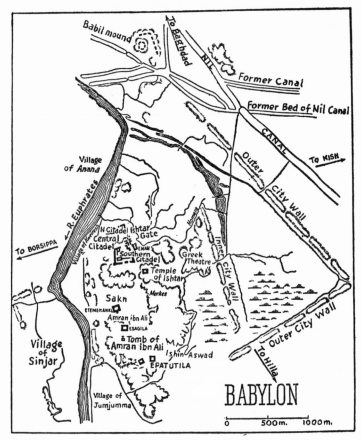

II. The site of Babylon (A. Parrot, Ziggurats et Tour de Babel, *fig. 40)*

which, indeed, according to the guides, were so infested with snakes and scorpions that it was not possible to visit them. However, he does mention the palace of Nebuchadrezzar and the furnace, into which were thrown the three young men, Hananiah, Mishael and Azariah, who had entered the king's service (Dan. 1.19; 3.21).[1]

Among later visitors were the Bavarian knight Schiltberger (about 1400), the Swabian doctor Leonhart Rauwolf (1574), the enthusiastic Pietro della Valle (December 1616) who brought back to Europe some inscribed bricks collected at Hilleh, Father Vincent Marie of St Catherine of Siena (1657), the Dane Karsten Niebuhr (1764), the Abbé Joseph de Beauchamp, vicar general in Baghdad (1786), G. A. Olivier, a delegate of the Convention (1794).[2]

The beginning of the nineteenth century saw a great access of interest in the Middle East and particularly in Babylon. A number of residents, agents of the India Company, and high-ranking political officers were seized with a passion for ruins when they realized that what was hidden underground was

[1] This is of course apocryphal. According to W. Andrae, *Babylon*, p. 224, Koldewey took a mischievous delight in conducting members of a fundamentalist sect to sites which he called 'the den of lions', the 'fiery furnace', but which were clearly not authentic. But the visitors wanted to 'see everything'. They were even shown the wall on which the mysterious hand had written the memorable words: *mené, teqel, perés* (Dan. 5.26–8).

[2] For further details about these and later explorers see the author's *Archéologie mésopotamienne*, I, pp. 13–35.

even more important than what was visible on the surface. Imaginative sketches gave place to exactly measured descriptions and a more systematic investigation whereby rumour and hearsay were sifted by means of personal control and an objective approach. These were the methods employed by C. J. Rich (1811, 1812, 1821), J. S. Buckingham and Bellino (1816), Ker Porter (1818), Captain Robert Mignan (1827), J. Baillie Fraser (1834), Chesney (1838), Coste and Flandin (1841) who produced a plan of Babylon, Lottin de Laval (1847) who invented a method of stamping clay.

In 1850 Layard made a few soundings—very limited in extent—at Bâbil, Kasr, and Amrân-ibn-Ali,[1] but the first systematic excavation of Babylon was undertaken by the 'Scientific and artistic expedition to Mesopotamia and Medea', which was directed by Fulgence Fresnel, the French consul, and in which an assyriologist, Jules Oppert, and an architect, Felix Thomas, also took part.[2] This expedition began in July 1852 and ended four months later in November of the same year. Forty-one crates of objects gathered from the excavations disappeared in

[1] From 7 to 9 December, 1850, S. A. Pallis, *The Antiquity of Iraq*, p. 351.
[2] J. Oppert, *Expédition scientifique en Mésopotamie exécutée par ordre du gouvernement de 1851 à 1854.* Vol. I: *Rélation du voyage et résultat de l'expédition* (1863). Vol. II: *Déchiffrement des inscriptions cunéiformes* (1859). *Atlas,* with text by Oppert and drawings by Thomas. Pietro della Valle worked alone at Bâbil (1616). Beauchamp had three assistants (1784), Rich had ten (1811), Pallis, *op. cit.,* p. 267.

the Tigris when the ship in which they were carried was wrecked at Korna in May 1855.[1]

If nothing more had been done, scarcely anything would have been known of Babylon. Fortunately the Deutsche Orient Gesellschaft, founded in Berlin in 1898, determined to carry out a systematic exploration under the direction of an architect, Robert Koldewey. He was assisted by a number of collaborators, most of them architects, and started work on the site on 26 March 1899. These archaeologists worked without interruption, summer and winter, for eighteen years.[2] Excavation only came to an end in 1917 during the First World War when the British advanced into Mesopotamia. Koldewey left, broken down in health, having struggled for years, according to W. Andrae, one of his closest collaborators, against the rigours of the climate, the intractable harshness of the site, and the opposition of assyriologists in Berlin.[3] He died in Berlin in 1925, having prepared, either by himself or in collaboration, several volumes[4] in which are recorded the findings of an expedition which, besides being extremely well equipped, had perfected a technique of excavation which was to be an example to many later investigators.

[1] *Archéologie mésopotamienne*, I, pp. 80–4.

[2] *Ibid.*, p. 177

[3] W. Andrae, *Babylon. Die versunkene Weltstadt und ihr Ausgräber, Robert Koldewey*, p. 212.

[4] See the Bibliography, p. 158 below.

The site[1] was particularly difficult because the mounds were widely scattered. The Bâbil mound (also called Mujelibe) is the first to be encountered when approaching from the north. It rises about 72 ft above the level of the plain (fig. III) and is roughly square with sides 270 yards long. Considerable quantities of bricks had been removed and used as build-

III. Bâbil-Mujelibe mound (Ziggurats, *fig. 3*)

ing material and when the archaeologists arrived they found only an accumulation of rubbish. It was possible, however, from inscriptions, to identify the remains of the summer palace of Nebuchadrezzar II (605–562 B.C.) which was protected by a wall, traces of which were found on the north and east.

[1] Besides detailed studies there are two comprehensive volumes on Babylon: R. Koldewey, *Das wiedererstehende Babylon* (referred to in the present work as *WEB*) and E. Unger, *Babylon. Die heilige Stadt nach der Beschreibung der Babylonier*. Also by Unger, the article 'Babylon' in *RLA*, pp. 330–69. A summary of the findings is given in *Archéologie mésopotamienne*, I, pp. 176–200.

The city itself is about a mile or more to the south on the site which is now known as the Kasr (castle). It extends for rather more than a mile along the bank of, or not far away from, the river, to the modern village of Jumjumma. It is clear that the course of the River Euphrates is now farther west than in ancient times when it flowed more or less through the centre of the complex of buildings which constituted the city. But the palaces, and almost all the temples—fifty-three have been counted—lay in the eastern section.

The excavation revealed only 'Chaldean' Babylon —that is, the last epoch in the city's history—and it was the impressive monuments of that era which were first brought to light by the archaeologists. This is the city of Nebuchadrezzar, the conqueror of Jerusalem (sixth century B.C.), which we shall now briefly describe.

Babylon was enclosed by a double system of encircling walls.[1] The inner rampart (fig. IV) was formed of two adjacent walls of crude (i.e. unbaked) brick: Imgur-Enlil, the inner wall, was 6·50m in thickness and was reinforced with towers; Nimid-Enlil, the outer wall, also reinforced by towers, was 3·72m in thickness. Outside this double wall, and separated from it by a distance of about twenty metres, a quay-wall of burnt bricks set in bitumen

[1] E. Unger, *Babylon*, pp. 59–64; F. Wetzel, 'Die Stadtmauern von Babylon' (*WVDOG*, 48).

rose above a canal fed by the Euphrates. This defensive system was completed by an additional, thinner, line of brick-work,[1] which was inserted *between* the two more massive walls. This barrier protected the city at close quarters and extended over a distance of about four miles. Several kings claimed to have had a share in its construction, among them Esarhaddon, Ashurbanipal and, of course, the Neo-Babylonian rulers Nabopolassar, Nebuchadrezzar, and Nabonidus. But the credit for initiating the work belongs to the kings of the first dynasty, Sumu-abum, Sumu-la-ilu, and Apil-Sin (ninteenth century B.C.) who also had a care for the security of their capital.

The outer rampart (*dûru dannu* or strong wall) was built on the east bank of the Euphrates (fig. V). This was entirely the work of Nebuchadrezzar; it defended his palace on the extreme north ('Bâbil') and extended over about seventeen miles. The area it enclosed was therefore of considerable size. It was intended to provide protection, in time of war, for fugitives from the neighbourhood who pitched their tents in the shelter of the walls. Here also there are two walls juxtaposed; the inner one of crude bricks, 7·12m in thickness with towers; the outer, of baked bricks, consisting of two structures fitted together and interlocking (7·80m and 3·30m).

According to the documents eight gates gave access to the interior of the city.[2] Four of these have been

[1] *RLA*, p. 335.   [2] E. Unger, *Babylon*, pp. 65–77.

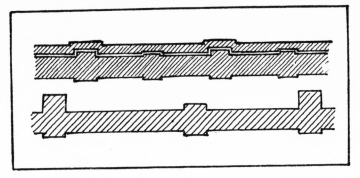

IV. The walls of Babylon (from Unger, Babylon, *Pl. 7, fig. 11)*

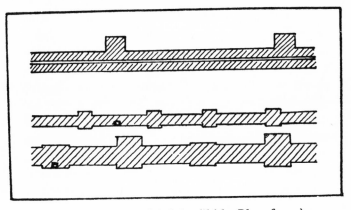

V. The outer wall of Babylon (ibid., *Pl. 7, fig. 10)*

discovered and excavated: the Ishtar gate on the north; Gishshu (or Marduk), Zababa (or Ninurta) on the east; Urash on the south. Four others can almost certainly be located: Sin on the north, Enlil and Shamash on the south and Hadad on the west,

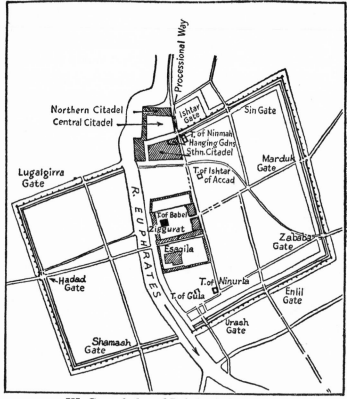

VI. General plan of Babylon (ibid., Pl. 2)

[26]

the last two in the 'new town' on the right bank of the Euphrates. These are the great gates (*abullu;* Sumerian, KA-GAL), which must be distinguished from the smaller entrances (*babu;* Sumerian, KA) known as Bel, Kellek, Lugalgirra, Mushepishi (magicians?), and the processional gate, the sites of which are almost impossible to identify.

The traveller who approaches Babylon from the north will come first to the site known to-day as Kasr (fig. VI), an area some 550 yards long, from north to south, and 430 yards wide, where the archaeologists started their excavations. In this sector they discovered a great complex of buildings to which were attached strong defensive fortifications. In their final state these structures probably date from the Neo-Babylonian era, but successive kings had a hand in their building and it is not always easy to distinguish their work with any exactitude.

Just before passing the inner rampart, the lay-out of which has been described above, a visitor to the city would enter the stone-paved processional way on either side of which stood high brick walls—on the west side those of the Northern and Central Citadels and on the east a fortification.[2] The processional way was decorated with figures of lions in enamelled brick (fig. VII).

[2] R. Koldewey and F. Wetzel, 'Die Königsburgen von Babylon, I. Die Südburg, II. Die Hauptburg und der Sommerpalast Nebukadnezars in Hügel Babil' (*WVDOG*, 54 and 55).

VII. Lion from the processional road (A. Parrot, Archéologie Mésopotamienne, *I, fig. 38)*

The Northern and Central Citadels formed a system of fortifications outside the city walls, apparently intended to provide additional defences for the southern palace which lay within the city. These buildings, though their remains are impressive, have the appearance of appendages. The Central Citadel, indeed, seems to have been a kind of museum in which were collected together a number of objects of very different dates, none of them of Babylonian origin; these were in fact trophies, spoils of war brought back by victorious kings. Some of the most characteristic and best authenticated items may be mentioned:[1]

[1] All these monuments are reproduced in Unger, *Babylon*, Plates 37–40.

A stele of the god Teshub with a Hittite hiero-
glyphic inscription, probably from Zendjirli
(seventh century B.C.).

Statues of Puzur-Ishtar, governor of Mari (beginning of the second millennium B.C.).

A relief of Shamash-resh-usur, Assyrian governor
of Mari (tenth–ninth centuries B.C.).

Steles of Ashurbanipal, king of Nineveh (seventh
century B.C.).

An inscription of Adad-nirari II, king of Nineveh
(about 900 B.C.).

There is, on the other hand, no such certainty about
the basalt statue of a lion trampling on a man (fig.

VIII. Lion trampling on a man
(ibid., *fig. 20*)

VIII and Plate 6). This extraordinary work, which
represents a beast overcoming a man, does not seem
to be Mesopotamian in origin; it has been thought
to be Hittite. The problem has arisen again as the

result of Mallowan's[1] discovery at Nimrud of an Assyrian chryselephantine figure representing a lion savaging a Nubian. This scuplture is therefore still a mystery (Plate 3).

Some two hundred yards distant is the Ishtar gate[2] on which is inscribed '*Ishtar sâkipat tebishu*' (Ishtar who destroys his enemy). This gate is almost 40 ft high (fig. IX and Plates 4, 5) and in fact consists of two gates (P, P[1]) built into the city wall (E, E[1]). The whole structure comprises a façade, heightened by two towers, and two interior chambers, one lying across its width (S, north gate), the other extending lengthwise (S[1], south gate).

Unlike the processional way with its lions passant,[3] the Ishtar gate is decorated with several rows of animals placed one above the other, dragons alternating with bulls. It has been estimated that there were 120 lions along the processional way and 575 dragons and bulls arranged in thirteen rows on the gate. But they could not all have been visible at one time, for the level of the entry has been raised several times and as a result the lower courses of the building have gradually been buried. The whole structure appears to have been finished with battlements and topped

[1] Mallowan in *ILN*, 16 August 1952 (coloured plate).

[2] R. Koldewey, 'Das Ischtar-Tor in Babylon' (*WVDOG*, 32). There is a reconstruction of one of the gates in the Pergamon Museum, Berlin.

[3] There is a reconstruction in the Vorderasiatisches Museum, Berlin. One of the lions is in the Louvre, gallery IV of the Department of Oriental Antiquities.

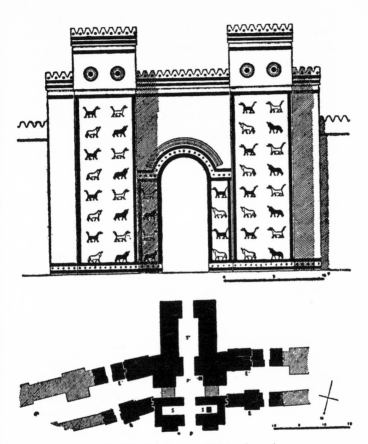

IX, The Ishtar gate (ibid., *fig.* 37)

with a wide frieze decorated with a design of daisies in enamelled brick. The prevailing colour of the decoration was blue; the animals were alternately blue and brown. The lion was associated with Ishtar, the dragon with a serpent's head (fig. X) was the emblem of Marduk; the bull (fig. XI) would have symbolized Hadad, the storm god. All this decoration was the work of Nebuchadrezzar.

Immediately adjoining the Ishtar gate was the temple of Ninmah, goddess of the underworld[1] (fig. XII). It was built by Ashurbanipal (668–631) and restored by Nebuchadrezzar (605–562) and by Awêl-Marduk (561–560). It is quite small (53·40 m. × 35·40 m.) but not without interest, owing to its being in a good state of preservation, and the ground-plan can be easily understood. The discovery of this temple was of considerable importance, for hitherto nothing had been known of the plan of a Babylonian temple.

The building had been very accurately orientated. The gate [1] opening to the north is flanked by projecting towers. A vestibule [2] leads to a court [3], the south wall of which, decorated with projecting pillars, indicates where the holy place would have been. There is indeed a doorway giving access to two rooms, lying across the width of the building, which were certainly an antechapel [4] and a chapel [5]; the latter has a *postament*, that is to say a raised dais on

[1] R. Koldewey, *Das wiedererstehende Babylon*, pp. 55-65.

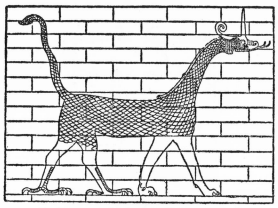

X. Dragon of Marduk (ibid., *fig. 38*)

XI. Bull of Hadad (ibid., *fig. 38*)

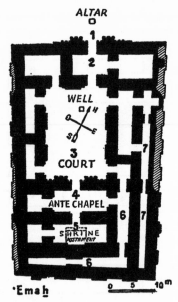

XII. Temple of Ninmah (ibid.,
fig. 39)

which would have stood a statue of the goddess. This
has disappeared for, being made of precious metal,
it would naturally have aroused the cupidity of
thieves. This was the extent of the actual shrine. In
addition there are living quarters for priests, and
long narrow corridors [6, 7] where it is possible to see
what may have been either the base of the stairways
or ramps leading to the roof, or a structure intended
to protect the chapel and its valuables from treasure-

[34]

seekers who might dig through the walls. The only other cult objects to be noted are a well in the court and an altar outside the temple facing the doorway.

No valuable objects were found, and the excavators had to content themselves with a few cuneiform tablets (one of which bore the name of an architect, one Labashi) and some very ordinary earthenware figurines of a naked woman with hands joined on her breast. The workmen found hundreds, if not thousands, of these on the site. It is not likely that these were images of the goddess who was venerated in this temple, or even of another divinity. They may possibly be effigies of a worshipper or of a sacred prostitute dedicated to the service of the temple, in accordance with contemporary beliefs, which seem very strange to us but which should be judged in the context of their time and their situation.

The processional way which, as has been indicated, started north of the Ishtar gate, continued south in a straight line for almost one thousand yards,[1] passing first alongside the great Southern Citadel, then the sacred precincts of the temple of Marduk, the city god of Babylon, dominated by the ziggurat E-temen-anki. Then turning at right angles in a westerly direction, it crossed the temple enclosure from side to side and ended at the bridge over the Euphrates. The road was 30–50 feet wide and was paved with lime-

[1] R. Koldewey, 'Die Pflastersteine von Aiburschabu in Babylon,' *WEB*, pp. 49–54.

stone flags set in bitumen. On the edge of each block is inscribed: 'I am Nebuchadrezzar, king of Babylon, son of Nabopolassar, king of Babylon. I have paved the road of Babylon with blocks of stone brought from the mountain (*aban shadu*=Lebanon?) for the procession of the great lord Marduk. May Marduk, my lord, grant me life for ever!' The central section of the road (6–7m wide) was fitted into an edging of breccia stone (*turminabanda*) conveyed by river from Til-Barsip.[1]

The road must have been constructed with particular care for it had to bear the weight of the huge statues of the god[2] which, on the occasion of processions, were drawn along it on chariots or floats.[3]

The processional way, as has been mentioned, skirted the Southern Citadel, a vast complex of buildings occupying the centre of the Kasr. This is the sector which has been most thoroughly excavated. It is bounded on the north by the Imgur Enlil wall, on the west by the Euphrates, though a great bastion lies between it and the river, on the east by the processional way, and on the south by the Libilhegalla

[1] Now Tell Ahmar on the middle Euphrates. It was excavated in 1929–1931 by the Thureau-Dangin expedition.

[2] According to Herodotus the statue of Marduk was about 10 ft high and made of gold; he states, however, that he has not seen it himself, but got the information from the 'Chaldeans' (*History*, I, 183).

[3] Cf. the reconstruction of one of these vessels in W. Andrae, *Das wiedererstandene Assur*, p. 41, fig. 21. There was a tiled fitting connected with this moving of the gods in the temple of Sin-Shamash at Ashur, W. Andrae, *op. cit.*, p. 156, fig. 67.

Canal. Even to-day this great mass of ruins is an impressive spectacle (Plates 2 and 3). All the kings of Babylon contributed to its building: Nabopolassar (625–605), Nebuchadrezzar (605–562), Nergal-shar-usur (559–556), Nabonidus (556–538). After the Persian conquest the Achaemenian kings added to it in their characteristic architectural style, but the essential portions of the structure were the work of Nebuchadrezzar and Nabopolassar.

The whole complex (fig. XIII) is trapezoid in shape, some 350 yards long (east to west) and rather more than 200 yards wide (north to south); it comprises five blocks juxtaposed from east to west, each including a

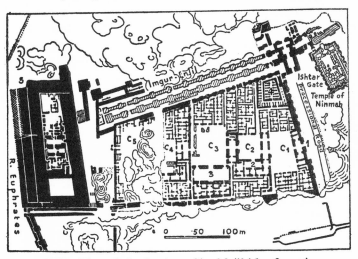

XIII. Plan of the Southern Citadel (ibid., *fig. 40*)

large court giving access to living quarters or reception rooms. The five courts [C_1–C_5], all different in size, lie more or less on the same axis, but the means of communication between them differ in each case.

The entrance [1] to the palace from the processional way was on the east. A vestibule led into the first court (66m×42m). The neighbouring buildings on the north and south are generally thought to have housed the garrison which guarded the royal residence. The second court [C_2] was approached through a double gateway; it was an oblong area (38m×35m) with more living quarters and a large reception room [2] on its south side (27m×9m). It is generally supposed that the officers who administered the kingdom occupied this block. A massive gateway gave access to the third court [C_3] the most imposing of all (60m×55m); to the south of this court lay what is called the Throne Room (52m×17m). Its external wall on to the court was adorned with a design in blue enamelled bricks incorporating a different set of motifs (fig. XIV): pillars surmounted by double capitals in the Ionic style[1] crowned with half rosettes and linked by garlands of palmettoes. On the frieze, a double garland of palmettoes, on the plinth a row of lions passant between a band of palmettoes and a line of rosettes. Inside the throne room, and facing the

---

[1] Koldewey's reconstruction, *WEB*, fig. 64, only shows two capitals one above the other. That by Wetzel in the Berlin museum, *Assur und Babylon*, fig. 36, has three.

XIV. Decoration from the throne room (from Koldewey,
WEB, *fig. 64)*

doorway, a recessed niche in the wall probably indicates the place where the king's throne stood.

Farther to the west lies a fourth court[C₄] of impressive proportions (34m×32m) with a reception room on its south side as well as what was no doubt the king's residence, the walls of which are noticeably thicker. It is tempting to conjecture that the harem or women's quarters were grouped around the fifth court [C₅], with additional reception and living rooms. Domestic staff must have been lodged in all the five areas, possibly in the northern section of each. Thus everything in this palace was characteristic of the pomp and magnificence of an eastern court, calculated to impress foreign visitors and at the same time to ensure the safety of the king who could only be approached through a whole series of screens.

At the north-east angle of the palace is most probably the site of one of the seven wonders of the world: 'the hanging gardens'. Indeed Koldewey discovered in this sector a vaulted, quadrangular structure (fig. XV) consisting of fourteen narrow chambers symmetrically placed either side of a long corridor [4]. The whole (42m×30m) was enclosed on the north and east by a massive wall, separate from the palace enclosure close by. On the south and the west lay a series of small rooms, obviously annexes to the central structure (Plate 2).

Diodorus of Sicily, Strabo, and Quintus Curtius have all described, in greater or less detail, this

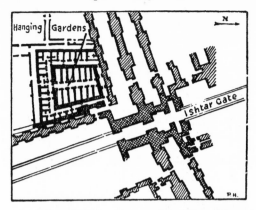

XV. Plan of the hanging gardens (from Unger,
Babylon, *Pl. 30, fig. 49)*

achievement which traditionally has been attributed
to Queen Semiramis. More probably, however, Berossus is right in regarding it as the work of Nebuchadrezzar.[1] This king, in order to cement the alliance
with the Medes, married Amyitis, daughter of Astyages, and, to console the Queen for her enforced residence in the Babylonian plain, devised something to
remind her of the mountains and the vegetation of
Persia. In an angle of the palace, on terraces supported by massive arches, gardens were laid out at
different levels (fig. XVI) and carefully tended. By
means of mechanical hoists, which had been used in
the ancient world from very early times, water drawn

[1] The texts are given in Koldewey, *WEB*, pp. 96–8; there is a
translation in E. Unger, *Babylon*, pp. 329–37.

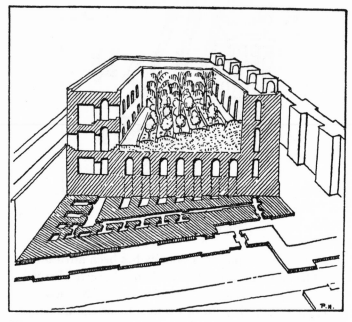

XVI. Reconstruction of the hanging gardens (from W. Otto, Handbuch der Archäologie, *III, p. 731*)

from numerous wells was raised to the terraces to
water the plantations. Thus, above the white roofs of
the city, the astonished eyes of visitors might gaze
on a green expanse of gardens[1] and marvel at the

[1] A reconstruction of the hanging gardens is given in W. Otto's
Handbuch der Archäologie, III, p. 731. See also J. Lacam's reconstruction in the *Revue horticole*, Sept.–Oct. 1949, p. 88 and his description,
pp. 123–7.

wonder, while, for the Queen, her distant homeland was brought near.

Between the western boundary of the Southern Citadel and the Euphrates, a huge fortification had been raised on the river bank, a formidable bastion built into the city walls and the quays. Nebuchadrezzar had erected it, he said, to protect Babylon and Esagila (the temple of Marduk) from the flooding of the Euphrates.[1] But probably it was not merely a dyke but an impregnable fortress, a last stronghold of resistance in the hour of danger.

To the south of the Kasr, in the direction of Amrân ibn-Ali, where to-day may be seen the three cupolas of the Mohammedan mausoleum in which are buried Amran the son of Ali and his seven companions who fell at the battle of Kerbele (A.D. 680), lies a site which the Arabs call Sakhn (the pan). Here lay the sacred precincts, south-west of which rose the ziggurat of Babylon.[2] This was closely connected with the temple of Marduk, Esagila, the precincts of which extended farther to the south; here was the most sacred sector of the city, the domain of Marduk its chief god.

The area may be seen as two separate but interdependent parts (fig. XVII). The first includes the ziggurat, E-temen-anki (the House of the Foundation-stone of Heaven and Earth), which dominates a

[1] Unger, *Babylon*, p. 63.

[2] The following description is a summary of the account given in the author's *The Tower of Babel*, pp. 46–50. More details are given in *Ziggurats et Tour de Babel*, pp. 70–88.

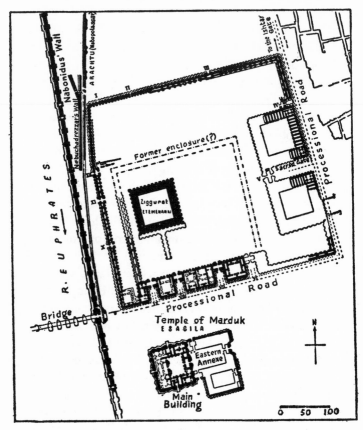

XVII. Plan of the precincts of E-temen-anki (Ziggurats, *fig. 41*)

trapezoid court measuring on the north, 460.20m, on the east, 408.75m, on the south 456.95m. on the west, 412.73m. Twelve gates open on to the precincts: three on the north (I–III), two on the east (IV, V) including the main gate (V), four on the south (VI–IX) and three on the west (X–XIII). On the south side were the apartments of the priests; storehouses and depositories were placed on the east in the form of large khans grouped round a central court in the angles of which there may have been chapels.[1]

Gateway V, the ceremonial gate, is probably that known as the 'holy gate' (*bâbu ellu*).[2] It opened on to the sacred way and it is easy to imagine the processions which must have passed through it. It is possible that this entrance was also known as the 'closed gate' (*dalat parku*). In fact, this gate was only used in the sixth month of each year, from the fourth to the sixth day, for the procession of Marduk and Nabu, and was afterwards closed again.[3]

South-west of the sacred enclosure rose the zig-

---

[1] Unger's interpretation. Wetzel and Koldewey consider them to be priests' lodgings.   [2] Unger's opinion (*Babylon*, p. 201).

[3] Unger puts forward this suggestion (*Babylon*, p. 202), which recalls the ceremony of the Porta Sancta of St Peter's, Rome, which is opened every twenty-five years and remains open for one year, after which it is closed again for twenty-five years. Similarly there are triumphal gates designed for the passage of kings or military heroes, such as the golden gate at Kiev, the gate to the Kremlin in Moscow; at Constantinople; in Rome (Arch of Titus, of Septimius Severus, of Constantine); in Paris (St Denis, St Martin, arch of the Carrousel, and Étoile); in London, though the purpose is not the same, the Marble Arch; in Berlin, the Brandenburg gate, etc.

gurat.[1] When excavations were carried out, from
11 February to 7 June 1913, nothing was found but
ruins, the site having previously been plundered for
building materials. The fundamental data on which
to base a reliable reconstruction of this monument
(fig. XVIII), which is undoubtedly referred to in the
Biblical account of the Tower of Babel (Gen. 11.1–9),
are the findings of archaeologists supplemented by
very valuable epigraphical material: the so-called
Esagila tablet which G. Smith saw in the nineteenth
century, which was rediscovered in a private collection and published by Father Scheil and which has
been acquired by the museum of the Louvre (AO,
6555).[2] To these may be added published material
on other ziggurats which are in a better, or even a
good state of preservation, such as those at Ur, Uruk,
Aqarquf and, the most recent, that of Tchoga
Zambil.[3] Finally, it would be a mistake to regard

[1] F. Wetzel and F. H. Weissbach, 'Das Hauptheiligtum des Marduk in Babylon, Esagila und Etemenanki' (*WVDOG*, 59); R. Koldewey, *WEB*, pp. 179–93; 200–10. E. Unger, *Babylon*, pp. 191–200.

[2] For the Esagila tablet see the author's *Ziggurats et Tour de Babel*,
pp. 22–8 and the bibliography, p. 22, note 16. Also Scheil's 'Esagil
ou le Temple de Bêl-Marduk à Babylone', in *Mémoires de l'Académie
des Inscriptions et Belles-Lettres*, XXXIX, pp. 293–308. The tablet is to
be seen in the Louvre, Department of Oriental Antiquities, gallery
IV, case 4. For notes on the text, see the author's *The Tower of Babel*,
pp. 20–2.

[3] For the first three see *Ziggurats et Tour de Babel*, pp. 129–44
(Ur), 121–9 (Uruk), 98–101 (Aqarquf). For the last see R. Ghirshman
in *ILN*, 6 Dec. 1952, pp. 954–5; 8 Aug. 1953, pp. 226–7; 3 July 1954,
pp. 13–15; 25 June 1955, pp. 1140–1; 8 Sept. 1956, pp. 387–9; in
Arts asiatiques, I (1954), pp. 83–95; II (1955), pp. 163–77; in *Archaeology*, 8 (1955), pp. 260–3.

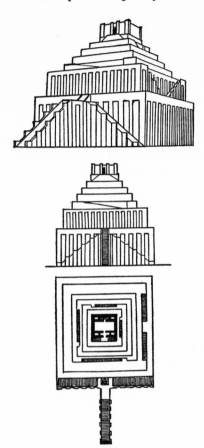

XVIII. Reconstruction of the 'Tower of Babel' (from Busink, De babylonische Tempeltoren, Pl. XI)

[47]

the account given by Herodotus[1] as entirely unworthy of credence. It is being increasingly recognized today that his observations are often valuable and the traditions he records are not always baseless.

From these various sources of information it appears that the core of the tower, made of crude bricks, was encased in a facing of baked bricks 15m thick. Its base was square, each side measuring slightly more than 91m (*c.* 130 yards). It seems certain that the ziggurat had eight storeys and that a small temple (*shaharu*) stood on the top. The means of ascent to the upper storeys are not exactly known, since it is not easy to reconcile the archaeological evidence with the inscription on the Esagila tablet and the description given by Herodotus. A stairway, built perpendicularly against the face of the wall, led either to the first (Busink)[2] or the second storey (Martiny, Unger, Dombart),[3] or perhaps even to the top (Andrae, Moberg)[4]; according to almost all the sources, two flanking stairways led as far as the first storey, the ascent being continued by ramps or stairways laid sideways and leading from one storey to the next (this would be the circular stairway mentioned by Herodotus).[5] From inscriptions dating from Nebu-

[1] *History*, I, 181.

[2] T. A. Busink, *De babylonische Tempeltoren*, Plate XI; the author's *The Tower of Babel*, p. 39, fig. VIII.

[3] *Ziggurats et Tour de Babel*, pp. 186–92.

[4] *Ibid*, p. 189, figs. 138, 142.

[5] *History*, I, 181. The passage is translated in Unger, *Babylon*, p. 326.

1. *Babylon and the Tower of Babel* (*Reconstruction by E. Unger*, Babylon)

2. *Site of the remains of Babylon: The 'hanging gardens'*

3. *Site of the remains of Babylon: East front of the Southern Citadel*

chadrezzar it appears that the temple at the summit was faced with blue enamelled bricks. The height of the whole structure cannot be exactly estimated, but it was probably 90m (*c.* 300 feet) or more. It is not difficult to imagine the impression made on strangers and pilgrims, not only by the numerous inscriptions couched in most grandiloquent terms[1] but by the soaring structure itself, witness to the might of the kings and the bold imagination of its builders (Plate 1).

Not only did the tower dominate the white expanse of the roofs of the town, it also over-shadowed the temple Esagila (house of the uplifted head), the shrine of Marduk.[2] This has only been partially excavated, for Koldewey located it at a depth of some twenty metres beneath the mound Amrân ibn-Ali. It was not possible to remove such a mass of debris, and the work had to be carried out by tunnelling galleries. As a result of the work done it has been possible to reconstruct the ground-plan.

[1] An inscription by Nabopolassar (625–605) runs: 'The Lord Marduk commanded me concerning Etemenanki, the stepped tower of Babylon, which before my time had fallen into decay and ruin, to establish its foundation in the heart of the underworld and make its summit like the heavens.' Nebuchadrezzar (605–562), asserting that his father had not been able to finish his plans, takes the credit for having carried them out successfully. 'All the peoples of many nations . . . I put to work on the building of Etemenanki. . . . The high dwelling of Marduk my Lord I placed at its summit. . . . I beautified the pinnacle of Etemenanki with splendid bricks of blue enamel.'

[2] Koldewey, *WEB*, pp. 200–10, with a picture of the excavations, p. 207, fig, 129; F. Wetzel and F. Weissbach, 'Das Haupttheiligtum des Marduk in Babylon, Esagila und Etemenanki' (*WVDOG*, 59); E. Unger, *Babylon*, pp. 165–90.

Esagila is first mentioned by Dungi (Shulgi)[1] of the third dynasty of the kings of Ur (twenty-second–twenty-first centuries B.C.); most of the successive kings of Babylon lavished care and devotion on it, as did the foreign rulers who later exercised sway over the city, with the exception of Sennacherib (704–681) who, on the contrary, distinguished himself by an orgy of destruction. The Neo-Babylonian kings, however, were the most zealous in their attentions. Both Nabopolassar and Nebuchadrezzar never tired of proclaiming themselves in countless inscriptions on bricks, 'the benefactors of Esagila and Ezida'[2] (*zani Esagila u Ezida*). Even after the city fell before the attacking Achaemenians the cult persisted into the first century B.C.,[3] so great was the veneration in which the god was held in spite of political upheavals.

The temple Esagila (figs. XIX, XX) comprised two structures placed side by side: to the west, a rectangular structure (the main building 10.80m × 79.30m) the east side of which adjoins another group of buildings (the eastern annexe) covering a considerably larger area (116m × 89.40m), of which only the external walls have been traced with any exactitude. The Esagila has four gateways, one on

[1] Unger, *Babylon*, p. 27. Eastern Annexe in fig. XIX of the present book.

[2] Ezida was the temple of Nabu (son of Marduk) at Borsippa (Birs Nimrud). For this temple and its ziggurat see *Ziggurats et Tour de Babel*, pp. 59–68.

[3] The last reference dates from 93 B.C. (tablets of 219, Seleucid era), according to Unger, *op. cit.*, p. 168.

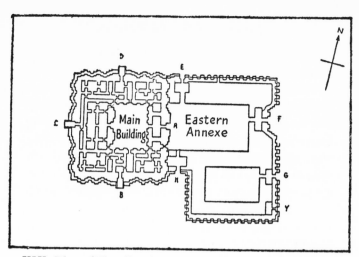

XIX. Plan of Esagila, the temple of Marduk (ibid., *fig. 44*)

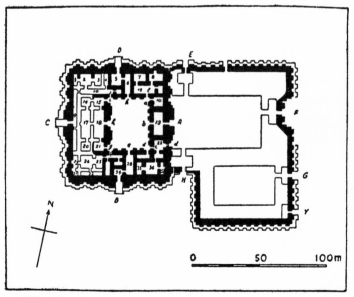

XX. Plan of Esagila, the temple of Marduk (ibid., *fig. 42*)

each side, but the eastern building has five, the principal one being on the east.

Esagila was described by the Neo-Babylonian kings as 'the palace of heaven and earth' or 'the palace of the lordship' (of Marduk); within it a number of chapels were dedicated to other deities whose iden-tity can be fairly well established. On a raised dais (*kisallu elinû*) stood the shrine of Marduk, the site of which can certainly be identified,[1] and those of Nabu and his consort Tashmetum.[2]

Others are indicated by inscriptions on a lower dais (*kisallu shapliu*). Here also were probably located the shrines of Ea,[3] of Nusku the god of fire, Anu the sky god and Sin the star of night.

No doubt the chapel of Marduk (40m × 20m) was the most richly decorated. Nabopolassar is said to have covered its walls with gypsum and shining asphalt(?). Nebuchadrezzar plated them with gold. The bases of the pillars were adorned with alabaster and lapis lazuli, the ceiling was of cedar-wood beams plated with gold, the panelling was enriched with precious stones.

[1] No. 17 in the plan. The shrine of Marduk's consort, Zarpanit, would have been in chamber 21 (Weissbach's suggestion).

[2] Nos. 35 and 37 on the plan, according to Weissbach: but Kolde-wey assigns these to Anu and En-lil.

[1] No. 12 where Koldewey found the site of a throne and clear traces of goddesses with flowing vases, the head of a dragon, and a fish, obvious attributes of the god Ea. When Alexander was dying, his generals came to this shrine to consult the goddess (who was said to have healing powers and whom they identified with Serapis) as to whether they should bring him there.

According to the documents, the god was provided with a bed and a throne. The bed was placed in a chamber known as 'the house of the bed' (*bît irshi*);[1] it was 4m 50×2m in size,[2] and was made of wood plated with gold. The throne was close by. According to an inscription of Ashurbanipal it was 1.66m high and 0.83m wide. Herodotus[3] mentions a statue representing the god seated. This statue was taken out of the chapel on occasions, and carried on a chariot in procession through the streets or in a barge for the ceremonial voyage on the Euphrates. Both chariot and barge were built of wood covered with gold or silver set with precious stones. There is no documentary evidence concerning the transport of the barge on a chariot.[4]

The statue of Marduk occupied an important place in the life of the city and the Babylonian state organization. At every celebration of the New Year festival the king of Babylon had to 'grasp the hand' of the god.[5] If, on account of internal or external troubles,

[1] It is extremely difficult to determine its location in the area excavated. An account of the different hypotheses put forward by Weissbach, Unger and Schott is given in *Ziggurats et Tour de Babel*, pp. 82–4.

[2] The dimensions are given in 'cubits', which may be taken as measuring 50cm. See Unger, *Babylon*, p. 178.

[3] *History*, I, 183. Cited in Unger, *op. cit.*, p. 327.

[4] Our word 'carnival' is derived from this practice. There is a reconstruction of a similar ceremony at Ashur in Andrae, *Das wiedererstandene Assur*, p. 41. fig. 21.

[5] A closely related ritual is depicted on a mural painting in court 106 of the palace at Mari, see M.-Th.Barrelet, 'Une peinture de la

the ritual could not be performed, the most fearful disasters were anticipated.

These monuments must have been destroyed or stolen in ancient days, for none of them have been recovered in the course of excavations. But we have some information about the iconography of Marduk from a collection of documents, the full importance of which became clear when they were classified. The most notable of these is a lapis lazuli plaque (*kunukku*) which was discovered during the excavation of Esagila.[1] The god is represented standing, the face in profile (fig. XXI). He is wearing a tunic scattered over with star-shaped discs and completely covering his body. From a chain round his neck three circular medallions, each decorated with a different design, hang down in front, the lowest touching the ground. On his head he wears a polos topped with feathers. In his right hand he holds the curved weapon known as a harpé, in his left a circle and a sceptre. His feet are not visible, but they are probably intended to be resting on the sea which is represented by wave-like lines at the base of the figure. Before him is the crowned dragon, the animal always associated with

cour 106 du palais de Mari', in *Studia Mariana*, pp. 9–35 and especially pp. 28–30; also, by the present author, ' "Ceremonie de la main" et réinvestiture', *ibid.*, pp. 37–40. For the New Year festival and the procession of the gods see E. Dhorme, *Les religions de Babylonie et d'Assyrie*, pp. 242–4; E. Unger, *op. cit.*, pp. 159–61; S. H. Hooke, *Babylonian and Assyrian religion*, pp. 56–62.

[1] Koldewey, *WEB*, p. 217, fig. 135; Unger, *op. cit.*, Plate 25, fig. 39.

XXI. Kunukku *with a representation of Marduk* (Ziggurats, *fig. 43*)

XXII. Kudurru, *with a representation of Marduk (from Unger,* Babylon, *fig. 37*)

Marduk. It is the emblem of Tiamat,[1] formerly his enemy but now pacified and become his ally.

This representation of the god differs very little from that shown on a *kudurru*[2] now in the British Museum (fig. XXII) which dates from the time of

[1] The female principle who personifies salt waters and, in the Epic of Creation, was the adversary of Marduk.

[2] A boundary stone on which rights to land were inscribed and which was deposited in a sanctuary. There is a considerable collection of these in the Louvre, in gallery IV of the Department of Oriental Antiquities.

Meli-Shippak II (twelfth century B.C.).[1] Here again he is long-haired, bearded and crowned, but his dress is a long robe with fringed flounces, and in place of the circle and sceptre he carries a mace. The horned dragon is there on guard. There are two additional objects: a double thunderbolt[2] and an iron implement with a triangular head (the *marru*), which is probably not merely a weapon but also a spade[3] such as is still used to-day by the local peasants.[4]

The iconography of Marduk displays a number of variants and presents some difficulties. On a cylinder in the Louvre[5] Marduk and his son Nabu are shown standing on dragons (Plate 8). They can be identified quite certainly by the emblems placed beside each figure: the *marru* for Marduk and the scribe's stylus for Nabu.[6] This monument would seem to illustrate the prophetic oracle: 'Bel (= Marduk) bows

---

[1] King, *Babylonian Boundary Stones*, Plate 21, British Museum No. 90827.

[2] This is generally interpreted as the emblem of Hadad, god of the elements and of storms.

[3] Thureau-Dangin, 'Marru', *RA*, xxiv (1927), pp. 147–8.

[4] In other words, the weapon of war can be converted, without any modification, into a tool of peace, and vice versa. This is the meaning of several passages in the prophetic writings: 'They shall beat their swords into ploughshares' (Isa. 2.4; Micah 4.3). In time of peril the tool could at once become a weapon: 'From your ploughshares forge swords!' (Hosea 3.10). So far as I know, no Old Testament scholar has pointed this out.

[5] Ao, 7217. Delaporte, *Catalogue des cylindres orientaux*, II, 686. It is made of chalcedony and measures 41 × 18 mm.

[6] Nabu, the god of Borsippa, was the god of writing and of scribes.

XXIII. Procession of gods from Maltaia (A. Parrot, Archéologie mésopotamienne, *fig. 8)*

down; Nebo (= Nabu) stoops; their idols are on beasts' (Isa. 46.1)[1] (Plates 8, 9 and 10).

Sometimes, however, the gods are represented simply by their emblems: the triangular spade and the stylus, either set in sockets or placed on the back of two, or even one dragon[2] (fig. XXIV). This simplification seems to bear witness to the very close relations which bound the two deities together so that their worshippers venerated them as one. Thus Isaiah mentions them side by side because so they were

[1] Scholars take this to mean that the defeated Babylonians attempted to save their gods by loading them on to beasts. But it may be suggested that the prophet also had in mind representations of the gods of Babylon standing on the animals which were always associated with them. Reference may be made to the cave drawings of Maltaia (fig. XXIII) and Bavian and to a number of steles which existed at the time of Second Isaiah.

[2] A cylinder in the Berlin Museum, A. Moortgat, *Vorderasiatische Rollsiegel*, 598.

XXIV. Nabu's stylus and Marduk's marru on a dragon (from Moortgat, Vorderasiatische Rollsiegel Pl. 71, fig. 598)

worshipped. Every year on the fifth day of Nisan (April), Nabu came from Borsippa to Babylon to take part in the Zagmuk and Akitu festivals. He had a place in his father's temple and, as already mentioned, the site of his shrine can be identified.[1] At the conclusion of the ceremonies he returned to his own house Ezida.

Together with Marduk and Nabu it would seem that the god Hadad also had a shrine in Esagila, judging by the lapis lazuli plaque which was found there. This was a votive offering made by Esarhaddon (680–99) and represents a silhouette of the storm god (fig. XXV). On his head is a calathos of feathers, in

---

[1] Chamber 35 of Esagila.

each hand he holds a thunderbolt, while his left hand also
grasps the ends of two leashes
issuing from the throats of two
beasts crouching at his feet. A
ziggurat five storeys high is
traced on his breast and three
large medallions, each decorated with a star, are placed
one above the other on a
long, pleated robe. The image
stands on a segmented base;
the thunderbolts are evidence
of the connection between
Hadad and the Canaanite
Baal, lord of storms and master
of the lightning.

XXV. Kunukku *with
representation of Hadad*
(Ziggurats, *fig. 13*)

To the east of Amrân ibn-
Ali, towards the lower ruins
of Ishin-Aswad (the black mound) Koldewey excavated two temples; one of these, which he was
unable to identify, he called temple Z; the other it
was possible to assign to the god Ninurta.

In its general plan (fig. XXVI) and orientation
temple Z[1] is similar to the temple of Ninmah[2] and

---

[1] Koldewey, *WEB*, pp. 218–23; Unger, *Babylon*, p. 141, considers
this to be the shrine of Gula, goddess of health.

[2] See above, pp. 32–5.

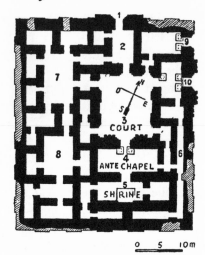

XXVI. Temple Z (Archéologie
mésopotamienne, *I, fig. 42*)

its essential features are the same: a main doorway on
the north [1], a vestibule [2], court [3], antechapel
[4] and chapel [5], and a long corridor all round it
within the outer walls [6]. The differences are certain additions: a wing on the west consisting of two
courts [7 and 8] and a number of chambers, and two
doorways [9 and 10] on the east front. Excavations
revealed several levels, the earliest some 9m below
the most recent, which suggests that the temple had
been in use for a long period of time. It did not seem
possible to determine the length of this period from
the depth of the different strata and Koldewey re-

fused to give an estimate, pointing out that in the Amrân mound 21m of debris represented 1700 years while at Merkes 6m of earth corresponded to the same period.[1]

The remains found there were disappointing: the model of a dove in baked earth and an apotropaic figurine. There was no indication of the deity to whom they had been offered.

*   *   *

A little to the east of temple Z another shrine (Epatutila) was discovered.[2] From the evidence of foundation cylinders it was assigned to Ninurta, the god of war. It was originally built by Nabopolassar and restored by Nebuchadrezzar who raised the floor level several times. The orientation is the same but the ground-plan differs from those of temple Z and the temple of Ninmah (fig. XXVII). The main entrance [1] is on the east, but there are two other doorways on the north [2] and the south sides [3]. The chief difference, however, is that there are three adjacent and communicating chapels [4, 5, 6] each with a doorway opening on to a central court and each having a dais. The central chapel is certainly that of Ninurta; the other two may have housed the god's consort Gula and his son, possibly Nusku.

The objects found here, while more numerous than those found in temple Z, were no more informative.

---

[1] Koldewey, *WEB*, p. 222.

[2] *Ibid.*, pp. 223–9; Unger, *op. cit.*, pp. 154–6.

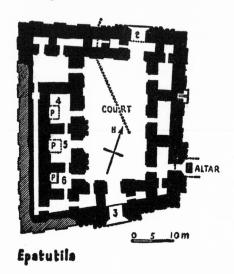

Epatutila

XXVII. Temple of Ninurta (ibid., *fig. 43*)

Some apotropaic figures were unearthed in foundation caskets at the angles of the doorways or in passages; figurines of a wide variety of types and of different dates; a male deity holding a vase from which a stream of water gushes, naked women, crouching apes, horsemen, a woman in a litter. All these are so varied that not much information can be gathered from them. There are some chronological indications, but they are contradictory. The god with the vase, for example, seems to date from the beginning of the second millennium, while most of the

[62]

votive offerings belong to the Achaemenian era (sixth to fourth centuries) or even to the Seleucid. In Parthian times the temple lay in ruins and was used as a burial ground, as were the upper strata of Amrân ibn-Ali.

* * *

A group of mounds to the east of the ziggurat is known as Merkes.[1] Excavations were carried out here in varying depths, sometimes as much as 12 metres. It was therefore possible to discover, with some precision, the relative levels of the buildings. The oldest strata could be dated to the first Babylonian dynasty (nineteenth to sixteenth centuries B.C.) on the evidence of cuneiform tablets. Nowhere else in the city was anything found of equal antiquity, but this does not mean that nothing existed, for there are references to Babylon in the twenty-third century B.C.[2] Water seeping in prevented the excavators from penetrating beyond certain levels, and thus so far back in time as had been successfully carried out at Nineveh for example.[3] In the Merkes mound (750m × 350m) the temple of Ishtar of Accad came to light, as well as sets of living quarters.

The temple of Ishtar of Accad (Emeshdari) was

---

[1] O. Reuther, 'Merkes. Die Innenstadt von Babylon' (*WVDOG,* 47).

[2] See above, p. 15.

[3] *Nineveh and the Old Testament,* p. 21.

discovered to the east of the processional road.[1] It
was rectangular in form (37.20m×31.07m) (fig.
XXVIII) and had two entrances—the main gateway [1] on the south, the other on the east—leading

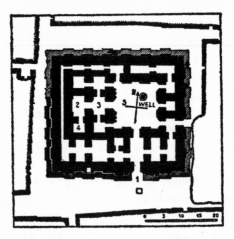

XXVIII. Temple of Ishtar of Accad (ibid., *fig.* 44)

to the inner court [5]. The most holy area is easily
identifiable. It consists of six chambers among which
the ante-chamber to the shrine [3], and the shrine
itself [2], with an adjoining service room, can readily
be recognized. Apart from some simplifications the
plan is the same as that of the Ezida temple at Borsippa. A foundation figure, representing a protective

[1] Koldewey, *WEB*, pp. 288–92; Reuther, 'Merkes', pp. 123–47;
Unger, *Babylon*, pp. 143–4.

4. *The Ishtar gate* (*Reconstruction by E. Unger*, Babylon, *frontispiece*)

5. *Babylon: The Ishtar gate*

6. *Babylon: The Lion of Babylon*

deity, was found under the dais in the shrine. There was also a well built of baked brick in the court and an altar in the road outside the temple and facing the main gateway.

The temple had been restored more than once, and finally by Nebuchadrezzar and Nabonidus. It was probably destroyed during the Persian era, for it is not mentioned in any texts after that date.

The Merkes mound was also the site of an extensive residential quarter. Though not strictly rectilinear, the streets were evidently laid out with an eye to order and harmony. The layout of private houses reproduces the fashion of the royal residences with

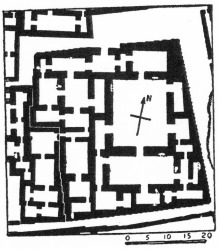

XXIX. Great house of Merkes (ibid., *fig.* 45)

[65]

apartments surrounding a central court. One mansion in particular attracted notice on account of its decorative architectural features, the façades being serrated like the teeth of a saw. This 'great house' had frontages on three streets, but only one entrance, and three of its walls were serrated in this fashion. The intention was, so doubt, to break the monotony of the bare walls which presented alternately an expanse of unrelieved light or shadow.

In this area great quantities of objects were found, as is generally the case when private houses are excavated, for these have usually not been rifled in ancient days as were temples and palaces, and thus are often more rewarding. Moreover, since it was the custom to bury the dead under their houses and to provide them with furnishings appropriate to the social position they had occupied in life, the excavation of tombs, when they are found intact, always reveals a large and frequently very valuable hoard.

Thus Koldewey and his collaborators collected several thousand small objects (pottery, figurines, tools, cylinders, tablets) which could readily be classified in well-known categories the date of which was definitely established.

*   *   *

The last item to be noted in connection with the exploration of Babylon is the mound known as Ishan el Ahmar (the red mound) or Homera, situated north-east of Merkes at the foot of the inner wall of the city. In the southern sector a Greek theatre was found.[1] The northern sector yielded nothing but a huge accumulation of debris. Koldewey attributed this to the works carried out on the site of the ziggurat at the orders of Alexander.[2] Before the tower was rebuilt, the material from the ruins had been buried some distance away. The death of Alexander put a stop to the work and his successors did not carry it on.[3]

[1] Koldewey, *op. cit.*, pp. 293–9.

[2] Strabo, XVI, 1, 5. Cited in Koldewey, *op. cit.*, p. 135; translation in Unger, *op. cit.*, pp. 329–30.

[3] Koldewey estimated the amount of debris at 300,000 cubic metres; this would correspond to the 600,000 working days mentioned by Strabo (10,000 workmen employed for two months).

II

BABYLON AND THE
OLD TESTAMENT

Babylon is first mentioned in the Old Testament as Babel, a form closely copied from the Accadian *bâb-ilu*; according to Genesis 10.10, Babel, with Erech, Accad, and Calneh[1] in the land of Shinar, formed part of the kingdom of Nimrod the 'mighty hunter before the Lord'. Although the Biblical text is of a relatively late date (ninth to eighth centuries B.C.) it embodies a much older tradition; Babel, with Erech (present-day Warka) and Accad (ed-Deir) is situated 'in the land of Shinar',[2] that is to say Babylonia. In Jer. 25.25; 51.41, the town is referred to as Sheshach,[3] but this is exceptional.

Although, as already mentioned,[4] the earliest archaeological traces of the city date only from the

[1] It is very probable that Calneh should be omitted. See Albright, 'The End of "Calneh in Shinar",' *JNES*, III (1944), pp. 254–5; *BASOR*, 131 (1953), p. 32.

[2] A phrase which recurs in the account of the Tower of Babel, Gen. 11.2.

[3] For an explanation of this name which is written as a cryptogram of the kind known as *atbash* see *Bible du Centenaire*, II, Jeremiah, p. 250, note *j*.

[4] See above p. 63.

first dynasty (ninteenth to sixteenth centuries B.C.) it is certain that Babylon was founded very much earlier. Koldewey reported stone implements[1] which he described as 'prehistoric' and which, even if they do not belong to such a distant time, certainly go back to various periods in the protohistory of Mesopotamia.[2] It is possible that Babylon was built by the Sumerians[3] and that its Sumerian name, Ka-Dingir-Ra, was literally translated as *bâb-ilu* by the Semites when they came in contact with the earliest inhabitants of the city. A Babylonian tradition records that Sargon, the Accadian Semite who founded the dynasty of Accad (twenty-fifth century B.C.), destroyed Babylon and carried away some of the earth from it to his capital, Accad, in order to endow it with a measure of the sanctity of the ruined city.[4] What indeed could be more holy than the spot where the *gate*[5] had stood through which the gods came to seek their worshippers?

Throughout its history, the independence of Babylon was severely tested. The city which was to give its name to a whole region (fig. XXX) and a civiliza-

[1] Koldewey, *WEB*, pp. 254-5.

[2] These have been discussed and described in the author's *Archéologie mésopotamienne*, II, pp. 107-331.

[3] Unger, *Babylon*, p. 26.

[4] *Ibid.*

[5] It should be remembered that *Bâb-ilu* means 'gate of God'. This etymology must determine the interpretation of the Biblical story of the Tower of Babel. See the author's Studies in Biblical Archaeology, No. 2, *The Tower of Babel*, pp. 16, 69.

XXX. Babylon in the Mesopotamian world

tion, and which, moreover, at least twice ruled all the
eastern world, was often and for long periods forced
to submit to overlords more powerful than itself. After
those of Accad, the kings of the third dynasty of Ur
(2124–2016) placed governors there; three of them
are known to us by name.[1] At that time the Sumerians of Ur had extended their hegemony across the
whole Mesopotamian basin as far as the middle
Euphrates,[2] but it was to collapse under the onslaught
of a fresh invasion of Semitic nomads, the Martu,

[1] Iturilu, Arshish, Murteli, see Unger, *op. cit.*, p. 27.
[2] The names of two of their 'governors' were discovered at Mari:
Niwar-Mer and Agishbilgi.

who later became sedentary settlers. The Sumerian kingdom fell and was unable to prevent the establishment of rival dynasties close to its capital—at Larsa and Isin—as it had been equally powerless to oppose the foundation of a dynasty at Babylon (about 1895) or the independence of Mari (about 2025). During this troubled period, and more precisely at the beginning of the eighteenth century B.C., may be dated the migration of the patriarchs and Terah's 'exodus from Ur' (Gen. 11.31).[1]

At that time Babylon was enjoying the prosperity from which her power was derived. The greatest monarch of the dynasty, Hammurabi (1792–1750),[2] had conquered all his neighbours in succession (Elam, Rim-Sin, king of Larsa, the State of Ashnunnak to the east of present-day Baghdad, Zimri-Lim, king of Mari), and was the unchallenged ruler of an empire stretching from the shores of the Persian Gulf to the middle Euphrates (as far as Aleppo) and to the upper Tigris (as far as Nineveh).

Paradoxically enough Babylon, his capital, provides little information about this monarch and his empire. It is rather in the vassal cities that we find evidence of that Babylonian civilization which left its mark on every aspect of life. Without any shadow of

[1] This will be discussed in a forthcoming study, *Mari and the Old Testament*.

[2] Evidence for this dating, which is one of the most difficult problems in Mesopotamian chronology, is given in *Archéologie mésopotamienne*, II, pp. 332–438.

doubt the 'age of Hammurabi' challenges comparison with the epochs to which the names of Pericles, Augustus and Louis XIV have been attached. The results of excavations throw light on all aspects of it, but here the achievements of Hammurabi as legislator may be considered. His Code bears witness to the regard for justice which inspired it. We know now that he was not the first to codify the law, and that several Mesopotamian kings before him had done something of the sort. But Hammurabi gave to his work a grandeur which his predecessors had not attempted. They wrote their codes on earthen shards; he caused his to be incised on a column of black basalt which was erected in a temple. Shamash, the god of justice, who dictated it to him, might indeed have exercised more supervision over its application.[1] He was not able to prevent such an impressive monument from being carried away as spoils of war in the twelfth century by the Elamite conquerors in one of those lightning raids by which Babylonia was constantly harassed.

A Hittite raid, about 1595 B.C., caused the final downfall of the first dynasty of Babylon.[2] Advancing from the Anatolian plateau, the army of Murshilish

[1] The Code of Hammurabi will be further discussed in *Le musée du Louvre et la Bible*.

[2] The dating of this raid depends upon the view taken of the whole chronological problem. Twenty years ago the date generally agreed on was 1806 B.C. (L. Delaporte, *Les peuples de l'orient méditerranéen*, I, p. 142), a much later date than the one previously adopted by Ed.

sacked the city but retired at once carrying with them the statues of Marduk and Zarpanit, the greatest of the gods of Babylon and his consort. They abandoned them at Hana on the middle Euphrates and returned to their own country, leaving the field open to other invaders—the Kassites to the north of Babylon and the 'sea people' to the south. We shall not go into the details of the interventions of the rival dynasties, since the story has no bearing on the Old Testament writings.

These wars and rivalries were, however, dominated by the rise of a third power, the Assyrians, with whom Israel, and later Judah, came into contact.[1] Tukulti-Ninurta I (1243–1207)[2] occupied Babylon and, to emphasize his victory, removed the statue of Marduk and took it to Ashur.[3] The power of the Kassites was declining, and in 1171 they were overthrown in a raid by the Elamites. It was not the Iranians, however, who laid claim to Babylon, but the Mesopotamian peoples—the Assyrians and the

Meyer (*Histoire de l'Antiquité*, III, p. 334), namely, 1926 B.C. Other scholars have suggested 1500 (Böhl) and 1650 (Goetze). The whole question is discussed in the author's *Archéologie mésopotamienne*, II, pp. 378–83.

[1] See *Nineveh and the Old Testament*.

[2] The dates given by E. Weidner, 'Die Königsliste aus Chorsabad', *AfO*, XIV (1941), p. 368.

[3] Unger, *Babylon*, p. 30, gives an account of the changing fortunes of this statue, which was carried off to Assyria by Tukulti Ninurta, sent back 66 years later by Ninurta-tukul-Ashur, recaptured by the Elamites in 1176 B.C. and taken to Susa whence it was recovered by Nebuchadrezzar I (1146–1123) who replaced it in its temple.

'sea peoples'. From the beginning of the ninth century the city was a vassal of the kings of Nineveh who ruled it either directly or through kings, theoretically independent but in fact subordinate and strictly controlled. Nevertheless there were upheavals, and on several occasions the vassals revolted and the Aramean rulers of the 'sea peoples' seized the throne of Babylon: Eriba-Marduk (802–763) founded a dynasty which was not brought under control till the time of Tiglath-pileser III, king of Ashur (745–727);[1] Marduk-apal-iddin II (722–711) was even more redoubtable and it required all the strength of Sargon II (721–705) to subjugate him.

He was a diplomat as well as a warrior. The Old Testament records the embassy he sent to Hezekiah king of Judah (716–687). 'About the same time, Merodach-Baladan,[2] son of Baladan, king of Babylon, sent eunuchs to Hezekiah [bearing] presents; for he had heard of the king's sickness and his recovery. Hezekiah rejoiced at their coming and took them to see all the house in which were his treasures, the silver, the gold, the spices, the precious oil, as well as the house of his armour and all his stores. There was nothing in all his palace and in all his dominions which Hezekiah did not show them.' (II Kings 20.12–13; Isa. 39.1).

[1] This king is mentioned in the Bible under his coronation name of Pûlu (Pul in II Kings 15.9) which he assumed when he was restored to the throne of Babylon.

[2] A fairly close adaptation of Marduk-apal-iddin.

This was by no means an official visit of courtesy as between one sovereign and another.[1] The king of Babylon was, in fact, engaged in organizing a coalition against his enemy, Sargon of Assyria, and was entering into relations with all those who might be persuaded to become his allies. Israel had disappeared, Aram no longer existed; it was therefore necessary for him to be on good terms with Judah— only a minor power, though Hezekiah set himself to enhance the prestige of his kingdom by displaying to the Babylonians his armour and his wealth. The story does not say whether they were impressed, but we are told of the reaction of Isaiah who presented himself at the palace without being summoned (II Kings 20.14–18). The prophet was well aware of the purpose of this secret diplomacy and endeavoured to dissuade the king from entering into any of these political and military alliances which could have no result, since the fate of Jerusalem was already determined.[2]

Though no pictorial representations of Hezekiah

[1] Cf. the visit of David's servants to Hanun, king of the Ammonites after the death of his father (II Sam. 10.2) or that of the envoys of Hiram, king of Tyre, to Solomon after the death of David (I Kings 5.1). On one of the El-Amarna tablets Pharaoh Amenophis IV writes to the king of Babylon: 'Could your brother hear that you were ill and not send his ambassador?'

[2] Jerusalem was to be destroyed at the hands of the Babylonians, not, indeed, by the king who was seeking the friendship of Judah at that moment, but by another ruler of another dynasty—Nebuchadrezzar—more than a hundred years later.

[75]

or his prophet exist, there is one of Marduk-apal-iddin (Merodach-Baladan). On a *kudurru* which is now in the Berlin Museum (Plate 7) [1] the king is shown receiving the homage of an official on whom he is bestowing a grant of land. The king, whose stoutness is not concealed by his long robe, holds a sceptre in his left hand and in his right an object which it is difficult to identify. [2] He has long hair and a beard and wears on his head a cone-shaped crown quite unlike that worn by the Assyrian kings. At the top of the plaque is a row of religious emblems, among which (from left to right) are the symbols of Nabu, [3] Ninhursag, [4] Ea [5] and Marduk. [6]

But in spite of all these intrigues, Marduk-apal-iddin had to fly before Sargon who, having 'grasped the hand of Bel', established himself on the throne of Babylon. His son Sennacherib (704–681) reigned in Babylon, sometimes in his own person, sometimes through vassal princes. The latter course, however, was not successful. To put an end once for all to these attempts at independence, the king of Nineveh re-

[1] VA, 2663, of black stone, about 18 inches high. Schäfer and Andrae, *Die Kunst des alten Orients. Die Kunst Vorderasiens*, 517.

[2] It may be a little rod used to flatten the nose in a ritual gesture.

[3] The stylus on the altar from which the horned dragon appears.

[4] The symbol *omega* placed on the altar has been the subject of much discussion. It may perhaps be the emblem of a fertility goddess.

[5] The crook with a bull's head on the altar from which emerges an ibex—two animals associated with the god Ea, god of water and of wisdom, but also father of Marduk.

[6] The triangular iron implement (*marru*) on the altar and the horned dragon.

[76]

turned to Babylon and savagely destroyed it (689 B.C.). He boasted of having brought the waters of the Euphrates through the city so that all the monuments made of crude brick, that is, of earth, were obliterated. The statues of the gods were removed to Assyria and Marduk was again made captive.

It is, however, most unlikely that Babylon could have completely disappeared; not even her conquerors could strip her of the glory which had been hers. Esarhaddon, the son of her destroyer, repaired the devastation wrought by his father and in 680 commanded that the city should be restored. What is the explanation of this reversal of a royal decision? There is reason to believe that Naqi'a, the widow of Sennacherib and mother of Esarhaddon, was a foreigner—an Aramean or a Jewess—and exercised considerable power. It is known that she was energetic and influential; a bronze relief, recently acquired for the Louvre (fig. XXXI), shows her close behind her son and thus associated with him in the government.[1] The inscription on this monument commemorates the return of the divine statues to Babylon,[2] where they were to enjoy new splendours, but also to suffer fresh tribulations.

[1] A. Parrot and J. Nougayrol, 'Asarhaddon et Naqi'a sur un bronze du Louvre', (AO, 20185), *Syria*, XXXIII (1956), pp. 147–60.
[2] In particular the statue of Ea. Marduk's statue was brought back to Babylon by Esarhaddon's son, Ashurbanipal, see J. Nougayrol, *loc. cit.* It may seem surprising that the principal god of Babylon was not the first to be recovered, but no explanation is forthcoming.

XXXI. Relief from Naqi'a (Museum of the Louvre)

On the death of Esarhaddon a bi-partite solution of the problem was attempted. The kingdom was divided between his two sons; Ashurbanipal ruled in Nineveh, Shamash-shum-ukîn took up residence at Babylon. The 'Babylonian Chronicles' have thrown much fresh light[1] on this period and revealed a number of hitherto unknown facts.

[1] W. King's *Chronicles concerning Early Babylonian Kings* (1907) was followed by C. J. Gadd's *The Fall of Nineveh* (1923), Sidney Smith's

Esarhaddon's decision to confer royal status on two of his sons proved to be fatal to Assyria, for the rivalry between Nineveh and Babylon became more violent than ever. Shamash-shum-ukîn rose against his brother Ashurbanipal, who retaliated with ferocity. Babylon was besieged (651–648) and captured, Shamash-shum-ukîn perished in the flames, and Ashurbanipal appointed Kandalanu in his place. The new king was at first submissive but later adopted a rebellious attitude[1] which became all the bolder when Ashurbanipal, who died in 631,[2] was succeeded by three much weaker kings: Ashur-etil-ilâni (631–628), Sin-shumulishir(627), and Sin-shar-ish-kun(627-612). The last of these was unsuccessful in his attempts to control the kingdom and failed to prevent Nabopolassar the Babylonian proclaiming his independence (November 22/23, 626) and founding a dynasty.[3]

Babylonian Historical Texts (1924), and D. J. Wiseman's recent publication, *Chronicles of Chaldaean Kings (625–556 B.C.) in the British Museum* (1956). This period is briefly summarised with special reference to those points where it bears on the Biblical narrative.

[1] E. Weidner, *AfO.*, XVI (1953), p. 310; M. E. L. Mallowan, *Iraq*, XVI, 2 (1954), p. 133; P. Pohl, *Orientalia*, 23, (1954), p. 266

[2] The dating of the Assyrian kings has been modified, see *AfO*, XVI (1953), pp. 305–10. Formerly the date of Ashurbanipal's death was taken to be 626 B.C.

[3] For Babylonian chronology see Richard Parker and Waldo H. Dubberstein, *Babylonian Chronology 626 B.C.–A.D. 45*; A. Goetze, 'Additions to Parker and Dubberstein's Chronology', *JNES*, III (1944), pp. 43–6; D. J. Wiseman, *Chronicles*, pp. 43–9.

This is generally known as Neo-Babylonian,[1] but it is also termed Chaldean. It lasted till 538, when Babylon was captured by Cyrus the Achaemenian, and included six kings who reigned in all for less than a hundred years. Incontestably the most famous of these were Nabopolassar and his son Nebuchadrezzar. We have already mentioned the magnitude of their achievement, not only in restoring its ancient glory to the city but also in raising all Babylonia from the ruin into which it had fallen. This was a period of great prosperity for the city and the State, in spite of continual military campaigns and expeditions. The whole eastern world, which for centuries had known only the law of Nineveh, now began to fall under the sway of Babylon. But this period was a brief one, for the dynasty established by the energy of the warriors Nabopolassar and Nebuchadrezzar came to an end with the ineffectual mystic Nabonidus, who was more fitted to be a hermit than a statesman.[2]

In a very short time events of great importance, with which Biblical history is closely connected, were to come to pass: the fall of Nineveh (612), the capture of Jerusalem (597), the destruction of Jerusalem (586), the capture of Babylon (539), the return and resettlement of the Jewish exiles. These events will

---

[1] Taking into account the first Babylonian dynasty, 1894–1595 B.C. (according to Sidney Smith's dating).

[2] In his book *Isaiah, Chapters XL–LV*, Sidney Smith attempts to rehabilitate him, but it is not an easy task.

now be considered in the light of the information made available by archaeological studies.

The decisive event for the Neo-Babylonian hegemony was the destruction of the Assyrian power. It is possible to study all the subsequent developments thanks to the tablet now in the British Museum (21 901) which was deciphered by C. J. Gadd.[1] This definitely dates the successive operations which led to the capture of Nineveh[2] in 612. In the course of these operations, which began in 616, the Babylonian forces under the command of Nabopolassar marched first into the region of the middle Euphrates (the Suhu and Hindanu district). Having reached the river Balikh[3] and pillaged a number of towns, Nabopolassar turned back to Babylon. The following year (615) he set out again, this time in the direction of the Tigris valley. He reached the Zab,[4] but was checked at Ashur, which he was unable to take. A year later (614) the town fell, apparently owing to the co-operation of the Medes led by Cyaxares. Nineveh gained a brief respite when the Babylonians had to

[1] *The Fall of Nineveh*. The text of the tablet was also published by D. J. Wiseman, *op. cit.*, pp. 11–20; 54–65, Plates IX–XII.

[2] See the author's *Nineveh and the Old Testament*, pp. 76–87. According to some scholars, for example Otto Eissfeldt, *Einleitung in das Alte Testament*, p. 468, Habakkuk's oracle (1. 5–10) refers to this period of history. The oppressors would be the Assyrians (2. 6–20) against whom the Chaldeans would arise.

[3] A tributary of the Euphrates entering the river on the left bank a little above the town of Raqqa.

[4] Tributary of the Tigris entering on the left bank.

move away to the middle Euphrates where a revolt (613) had been instigated by the Assyrians. Rabilu was taken but not Anatu.[1] The next year a concerted attack by Babylonians, Medes and Scythians[2] was launched. Nineveh was taken (August 612) and its king Sin-shar-ish-kun died when the city was set on fire.[3]

While the Medes returned home carrying away the best of the spoils, Nabopolassar pursued those Assyrians who had made their escape and were settled at Haran[4] with Ashur-uballit as their king. There was a reshuffling of alliances, such as frequently happens, and Egypt and Assyria joined forces. Pharaoh Psammetichus sent an auxiliary force, not only to save the refugees from being completely dispersed, but chiefly to contain an enemy whom he suspected of harbouring unlimited ambitions. But in fact Nabopolassar's westward drive was not checked. With the assistance of the Medes Haran was occupied after two campaigns (611–610, 610–609) and Ashur-uballit was forced to fly beyond the Euphrates. All his attempts to recover his temporary capital failed. The power of Assyria had come to an end. Hence-

[1] The present-day town of Ana built partly on an island in the Euphrates.

[2] Gadd (*op. cit.*, pp. 14–15) identifies these with the Umman-manda as does Dhorme in *RB*, 1924, p. 230. Wiseman (*op. cit.*, pp. 15–16), however, regards them as Medes.

[3] An episode in the history of Sardanapalus.

[4] The town mentioned in Gen. 11.31; to-day it lies in Turkish territory between the Euphrates and the Tigris.

forward there were only two great powers, confronting each other one on either side of 'the river':[1] the Egyptians lay at Carchemish on the right bank; the Babylonians occupied positions at Quramati on the left bank (fig. XXXII). The moment for the great clash of forces was at hand.

Meanwhile the little kingdom of Judah did not confine itself merely to waiting on events. King Josiah (640–609) tried to make capital out of the international situation. After the death of Ashurbanipal which, as we have seen,[2] marked the decline of the Assyrian power, Josiah threw off his vassalage and abandoned the subservience which his predecessors Manasseh (687–642) and Amon (642–640) had displayed. In 622 he embarked on a religious revolution, as a result, according to the Biblical narrative, of the discovery in 'the house of Yahweh of the book of the Law'.[3] In order the better to control it, he centralized the cult at Jerusalem, but his primary task was to cleanse the Temple and the city of everything which was defiling them—altars, statues of planetary deities, Canaanite idols, pagan cult ob-

[1] The Babylonian occupation of Kimuhu on the right bank of the river did not last long, and it does not appear that the forces which occupied Shunadiri, Elammu and Dahammu (the sites of which have not been identified) constituted a serious threat. See Wiseman, *op. cit.*, pp. 21–3 and the map on p. 22.

[2] See above p. 79.

[3] II Kings 22–3. Almost all scholars agree that this document was the book of Deuteronomy. See A. Lods, *Les Prophètes d' Israël et les débuts du judaïsme*, pp. 157–75.

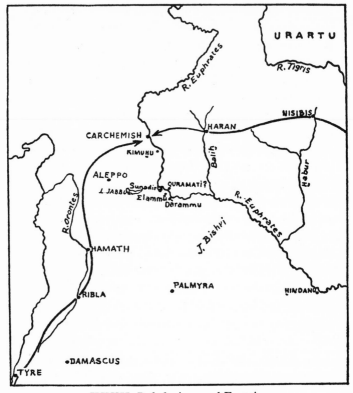

XXXII. Babylonians and Egyptians

jects. At the same time he ordered the destruction of all the high places in the land and the 'putting down' of all the priests who served them. Josiah was only twenty-six years old[1] when he had the courage to

---

[1] He had ascended the throne at the age of eight (II Kings 20.1).

initiate this 'reformation'. This is clear evidence, not only of his energy, but also of powerful allies. These he found among the prophets, Jeremiah in particular,[1] and also among the priests, whose interests were served by the regulation and official support of the cult. To the mass of the people, the pious king appeared as the champion of national independence, enjoying the favour of Yahweh and destined to restore the greatness of the nation. The fact that Josiah was able to carry his reformation into the former kingdom of Israel[2] is evidence, not that he was acting as the vassal of the king of Nineveh there,[3] but of the weakness of that monarch.[4]

Was Josiah's head turned by his success? It may be so, and that would account for his more than rash action in opposing the advance of Pharaoh Necho (609–594) who had left Egypt to 'go up against the king of Assyria on the river Euphrates'.[5] This is made clear from the Babylonian Chronicle. Necho was

[1] A. Lods, *op. cit.*, p. 165; *La religion d'Israël*, p. 151.

[2] II Kings 23.15–20, where mention is made not only of Bethel but of 'the cities of Samaria'.

[3] As maintained by W. F. Albright, *The Biblical Period*, p. 45.

[4] See the author's *Samaria*, p. 88, note 5.

[5] II Kings 23.29. In the old translations this passage has been taken to mean that Pharaoh was moving *against* the king of Assyria. But it is clear from the Babylonian Chronicle (BM, 21946) that this should be corrected, and that Josephus was drawing on a reliable tradition when he wrote (*Antiquities*, X, 5, 1) that Necho went to war 'against the Medes and the Babylonians who would have broken the power of the Assyrians'. Compare the account of these events in II Chron. 35.20–4.

going to the help of Ashur-uballit who had fled to Carchemish. Josiah tried to bar the way of the expeditionary force which, in order to avoid the peak of Carmel, had to cross the mountain range by the pass of Megiddo. He was killed at the outset of the battle

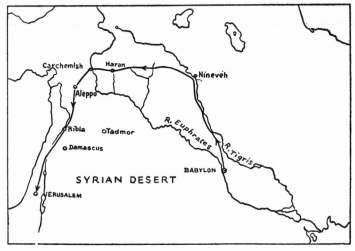

XXXIII. Babylon and the Middle East

and his troops took his body back to Jerusalem. His second son Jehoahaz (Yahweh grasps) was proclaimed king forthwith.[1]

Now the two adversaries were face to face—Egyp-

---

[1] II Kings 23. 30. It is, perhaps, surprising that the eldest son did not succeed his father. But his turn came soon afterwards, for Jehoahaz only occupied the throne for three months.

tians at Carchemish,¹ Babylonians across the river
(fig. XXXIII). The ageing Nabopolassar remained
in his capital, handing over the command to his son,
the crown prince Nebuchadrezzar.² Crossing the
Euphrates he gave battle; the Egyptians suffered a
total defeat³ and most of them were slaughtered on
the spot. The fugitives were pursued into the province
of Hamath where they met the same fate. In the
month of August 605 the victorious Babylonians
reached the Egyptian frontier.⁴ Nebuchadrezzar had
conquered 'all the land of the Hatti'—that is to say,
Syria and Palestine.

At Jerusalem, Jehoahaz had been dead for four
years; he had incurred the displeasure of Pharaoh
Necho who had summoned him to his headquarters
at Riblah,⁵ deposed him and installed his brother

¹ The modern town of Djerablous in Turkish territory. The site
has been excavated by several expeditions organized by the British
Museum from 1878 to 1920.

² The Hebrew form of the name is used here; the Babylonian
form is Nabu-kudurri-usur (Nabu guards my land-mark); the Latin
transcription is Nabuchodonosor.

³ This defeat had repercussions in Judah, echoes of which may be
found in Jer. 46.2.

⁴ Jer. 46.13. One of the oracles of Habakkuk (1.5–10) would apply
exactly to this situation: 'the Chaldeans, that bitter and hasty people,
which march through the breadth of the earth, to possess dwelling
places that are not theirs.' It would be true to say of them, when
they reached the Egyptian frontier, that 'he scoffs at kings and princes
are a derision to him: he derides every stronghold.'

⁵ The present-day town of Ribli, about 30 miles south of Homs on
the right bank of the Orontes. Nebuchadrezzar made this city his
headquarters during the siege of Jerusalem (II Kings 25.6). It was not
the first time that opposing armies were to choose identical sites for
their headquarters.

Eliakim (God exalts) in his place. Eliakim was made to change his name to Jehoiakim (Yahweh exalts).[1] The king of Judah had a new master, Nebuchadrezzar, whom he served with equal humility.

The king of Babylon could not stay long in his newly conquered territory. On the eighth day of the month of Ab (15/16 August 605) his father Nabopolassar died in Babylon; twenty-three days later the crown prince arrived at his capital. On the first day of the month Elul (6/7 September 605) he ascended the throne and became king of the most powerful State of the time.

This State, however, had to be very closely supervised. All the actions and operations of the king are recorded in the Babylonian Chronicle.[2] Every year Nebuchadrezzar had to send an expeditionary force into Syria and Palestine, not only to collect tribute but also to suppress incipient revolts. The king of Judah, after his first submission, tried to shake off the yoke, but appropriate measures were applied to bring him to a better sense of reality.[3] It is not certain

[1] Pharaoh thus displayed his authority. At a later date, Nebuchadrezzar acted in the same manner towards Mattaniah, causing him to change his name to Zedekiah (II Kings 24.17).

[2] Tablet 21946 in the British Museum. Details are given in Wiseman, *op. cit.*, pp. 28–32.

[3] II Kings 24.1–2. According to Paul Humbert, *Problèmes du livre d'Habacuc*, the oracle of the prophet in 1.5–11 refers to this period. The tyrant who was to be chastised by the Chaldeans is Jehoiakim.

whether his death in 598 was due to natural causes or to external agents.[1]

Jehoiachin succeeded him without any difficulties, but his effective reign lasted only three months.[2] The Babylonians intended to destroy the last of the small independent States. According to their custom, they mobilized their forces in December and reached Palestine in January 597. On the second day of the month Adar (15/16 March 597)[3] Jerusalem fell. The event is described in the Babylonian Chronicle and in the Bible as follows:

BABYLONIAN TEXT	OLD TESTAMENT
In the seventh year, in the month Kislev, the king of	At the return of the year, King Nebuchadrezzar

[1] The words 'slept with his fathers' (II Kings 24.6) simply mean 'died'. The passage in II Chron. 36.8, in the Septuagint version, mentions a burial in the garden of Uzzah, which suggests a customary form of burial. Jeremiah, on the other hand (22.19), announces that: 'He shall be buried with the burial of an ass: he shall be drawn and cast forth outside the gates of Jerusalem.' The passage in II Chron. 36.6 which records that Nebuchadrezzar put Jehoiakim in fetters and took him to Babylon either contradicts what is said in II Kings and Jeremiah, or else should not be taken literally. Nebuchadrezzar perhaps only *intended* to take the king to Babylon. See below, p. 119, in connection with the tradition in the book of Daniel.

[2] II Kings 24.8; II Chron. 36.9 (three months and ten days). The king was then only eighteen years old (or eight years, according to Chronicles).

[3] Until D. Wiseman (*op. cit.*, p. 73) had deciphered the cuneiform tablet in 1956 the exact date of the capture of Jerusalem was not known.

Accad gathered his troops together and advanced towards the land of Hatti.[1] He besieged the town of Judah[2] and on the second day of the month Adar he took the town and made the king prisoner.[3] He chose a king after his own heart,[4] took much tribute from him and sent him to Babylon.

brought him [Jehoiachin] to Babylon, with the precious things of the house of Yahweh, and he made Zedekiah his brother king over Judah and Jerusalem (II Chron. 36.10).

It would be difficult to find clearer confirmation of the Biblical narrative[5] which does not conceal the severity of the defeat. The fall of Jerusalem meant, not only the capture of booty, but exile for a whole category of its citizens (fig. XXXIV). The king was deported with his mother,[6] his wives, the officers of his household and of his army, seven thousand men able to bear arms and one thousand craftsmen (smiths and armourers).[7] The figures relating to this first

[1] A term for Syria and Palestine.

[2] Jerusalem.

[3] Jehoiachin.

[4] Zedekiah.

[5] II Kings 24.10–17; II Chron. 36.10. The account in Chronicles, which is shorter than that in Kings, is similar in style to the Babylonian Chronicle.

[6] Nehushta, daughter of Elnathan of Jerusalem, according to II Kings 24.8.

[7] Skilled metal-workers, to prevent surreptitious rearmament. The Philistines had done the same thing in the past, I Sam. 13.19–22 (see *Bible du Centenaire*, II Kings, p. 289, note *h*).

XXXIV. Deported population on the march (Nineveh and the Old Testament, *fig. XI.*)

deportation vary according to the different authors and traditions: eight thousand (II Kings 24.16), ten thousand (II Kings 24.14), three thousand and twenty-three (Jer. 52.28). The Babylonians were following the example of the Assyrians: the deportation of populations, the truncating of conquered States by imprisoning the upper strata of the people, the carrying off of booty. It is all explicitly recorded, both in the Biblical narrative and in the cuneiform text. To these should, however, be added an important note; the prophet Ezekiel was in the convoy.[1] The route by which he travelled to Babylon is not known[2] (fig. XXXV), but Assyrian reliefs give some idea of the long trek on which these refugees were taken,

[1] This is evident from Ezek. 1.2. According to M. Noth, *Histoire d'Israël*, p. 305, the prophet was not deported till 587 B.C.

[2] Possibly, however, he travelled across Palestine and Syria and then either along the course of the Euphrates or across northern Syria and Gezirah to the Tigris.

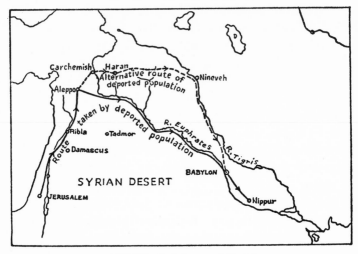

XXXV. Babylon and Judah

against their will, under a strong escort, with a small allowance of baggage, the men travelling on foot, the women and children carried in two-wheeled carts.[1] This first contingent was certainly dispersed on its arrival. The royal family remained in Babylon.[2] The prophet Ezekiel, with a considerable number of his compatriots, was given a residence 'beside the river Chebar'.[3]

[1] Reliefs in the Louvre, see *Nineveh and the Old Testament*, p. 47, fig. XI.

[2] See below, pp. 110–11.

[3] Ezek. 1.3a. The 'river Chebar' may be identified with the *naru kabaru* (the great canal) flowing from the Euphrates in the Nippur area south-east of Babylon, see below p. 124.

In the course of the campaign of 597, and while he was investing Jerusalem, King Nebuchadrezzar seized Lachish. The excavation of Duweir[1] revealed the destruction of one stratum of the town[2] which was due to this action. Lachish had previously been taken by the Assyrians,[3] now it submitted again to alien domination. Its position as a strong-point on the route from Egypt was so important that the Babylonians could not afford to neglect it. But once the storm had passed, Lachish, like Jerusalem, enjoyed a brief respite.

From the cuneiform texts the course of events can be traced up to 593.[4] It appears that the king of Babylon seldom stayed long in one place. The need for constant vigilance was always taking him out of his country, from which, however, he could not be absent for very long periods owing to unsettled conditions there.[5] On several occasions he came back to

[1] This identification is indisputable.

[2] Level III. According to the interpretation offered by Starkey and adopted by Albright, *BASOR*, 132 (1953), p. 46; Wright, *BA*, XVIII (1955), p. 15 and *JNES*, XIV (1955), pp. 188–9. Miss O. Tufnell, on the other hand, in *Lachish*, III, p. 55, considers that the third level was destroyed by Sennacherib in 701 B.C.

[3] *Nineveh and the Old Testament*, pp. 56–9.

[4] Wiseman, *op. cit.*, pp. 35–7.

[5] A cuneiform tablet dating from the eleventh year of Nebuchadrezzar's reign contains an account of a legal action concerning a certain land-owner of high rank who was sentenced to death for high treason (see E. Weidner in *AfO*, XVII (1954–55), pp. 1–9. This event may possibly be connected with the risings that Nebuchadrezzar had to suppress in the tenth year of his reign, Wiseman, *op. cit.*, p. 36

Syria; his last expedition into that country took place in the winter of 594/593. At this point there is a gap in the documentation; apart from two fragmentary texts which record an expedition against Egypt in 568/567[1] there is no information in Babylonian sources about the military activities of the king. It must be supposed that nothing had happened!

The new king of Judah, Zedekiah,[2] resented the condition of subservience which had been forced on him. A strong party in the kingdom urged him to make an alliance with Egypt, whose ruler Psammetichus (594–588) had been encouraged to adopt an aggressive policy as a result of his victory over Ethiopia. During his travels in Phoenicia (590) he was able to negotiate agreements with a view to organizing a general revolt.[3] It is not surprising that Zedekiah was tempted. The prophets, speaking as the mouthpiece of 'Yahweh of hosts, God of Israel', were proclaiming the downfall of Babylon and the return of the king and the captives.[4] This blind optimism, which was shared by most of the exiles, even though they were in a better position than others

[1] Nos. 33041 and 33053 in the British Museum, included in Wiseman, *op. cit.*, pp. 30, 94–5 and Plates XX–XXI.
[2] In Hebrew Ṣidkiyyāhu (Yahweh is my righteousness). He had had to change his name, at the order of his overlord; formerly he had been called Mattaniah (gift of Yahweh) (II Kings 24.17). Zedekiah was the son of Josiah and the uncle of Jehoiachin whom he succeeded, not his brother as stated in II Chron. 36.10.
[3] See E. Drioton and J. Vandier, *L'Egypte*, p. 596.
[4] Jer. 28.1–4.

to recognize the true situation,[1] was resolutely opposed by Jeremiah. Unceasingly, by action[2] as well as in words, he urged submission to the king of Babylon,[3] and wrote to the exiles using the opportunity offered by an embassy which Zedekiah sent to his overlord, no doubt bearing assurances of his fidelity.[4]

Nebuchadrezzar, however, was not deceived. In the ninth year of Zedekiah's reign[5] the Babylonian army appeared before the walls of Jerusalem. The siege lasted a year and a half,[6] except for a short interruption caused by the arrival of relieving forces sent from Egypt by the new Pharaoh Apries (588–568).[7] This diversion had no effect on Jeremiah, who continued to advocate surrender.[8] For this he was

---

[1] Jer. (29.21, 24) gives the names of several 'prophets' in Babylon—Ahab, Zedekiah, Shemaiah—who also were foretelling the downfall of the Babylonian empire.

[2] As when he put a symbolic yoke on his neck (Jer. 28.10.)

[3] Jer. 27.   [4] Jer. 29.1–23.

[5] II Kings 25.1. This was in 587, not 588 B.C. This dating, which is that of A. Lods, is supported by the very definite indications given in the British Museum tablet 21946 which fix the date of Zedekiah's accession at 597 (not 598), see Wiseman, *op. cit.*, p. 33. According to the Biblical narrative, the siege began 'in the ninth year of Zedekiah's reign' (II Kings 25.1, cf. Jer. 39.1). It may be noted that during the excavation of Lachish a tile was found inscribed 'In the ninth (year . . .)' (ostracon No. 29); it seems probable that this refers to a date in the reign of Zedekiah. For the Lachish ostraca see below p. 99–104.   [6] II Kings 25.2. From January 587 to July 586.

[7] The raising of the siege is mentioned only by Jeremiah 34.21 and 37.5.

[8] It will be shown later that an allusion to this activity is to be found in the Lachish ostraca, see below pp. 102–3.

put in prison, but he continued to have secret conversations with the king, who became more and more perplexed and anxious about the future course of events.[1] It is worth noting that, in the heart of Babylonia and therefore far removed from the scene of these events, Ezekiel placed no more faith than did Jeremiah in the power of Egypt and continued to foretell the victory of Babylon.[2]

Resistance was, however, coming to an end. When famine was raging in the city and a breach had already been made in the walls, Zedekiah left his capital by night and, passing through the lines of the investing troops, fled through the Kedron valley[3] to take refuge in the Jordan area.[4] He was observed, pursued, and overtaken in the plain of Jericho. The troops who were with him fled and he was made prisoner and taken to Nebuchadrezzar's headquarters at Riblah.[5] He was condemned as a criminal[6] and,

[1] Jer. 37.3–38.28.

[2] Ezek. 30.21–32.32. This passage says much for the speed with which news travelled even among those who, like Ezekiel, were not able to make use of official messengers.

[3] The way by which he left the city is exactly indicated: 'by the way of the gate between the two walls which was by the king's garden' (II Kings 25.4). The site can be identified with a fair degree of accuracy at the southern point of ed-Dehura, where excavation revealed the end of a stairway. Diagrams of the site are to be found in Vincent, *Jérusalem de l'Ancien Testament*, I, p. 85, fig. 32.

[4] The river Jordan lies about thirty-five miles away by road.

[5] Riblah served as headquarters for the Egyptians as well as the Babylonians. It commanded the road from Homs to Tripoli, a strategic route for military operations in almost any direction.

[6] II Kings 25.6. According to Ezekiel, the king had broken his oath and therefore had to be punished (Ezek. 17.11–21).

7. *Merodach-Baladan* (*Marduk-apal-iddin*)

8.

9.

10.

*Assyro-Babylonian deities, from cylinders in the Louvre and
the National Library, Paris*

XXXVI. Sargon II putting out the eyes of defeated enemies (Samaria, Capital of the Kingdom of Israel, *fig. XXIII*)

after he had witnessed the execution of his sons, his eyes were put out[1] (fig. XXXVI). He was then placed in irons and deported to Babylon.

Jerusalem was taken (586) and a number of important and influential persons among the inhabitants

[1] This form of punishment was frequently inflicted by the Assyrian kings, see *Samaria, Capital of the Kingdom of Israel*, p. 82, fig. XXIII.

were arrested at the orders of Nebuzaradan, 'a servant of the king of Babylon',[1] who, as his actions showed, had been given full authority. Some seventy prisoners[2] were taken to Riblah where Nebuchadrezzar had them put to death.

Of those who were spared, some—the wealthier of the inhabitants—were deported[3] (the artisans had left with the first batch of exiles in 597), others—peasants and humble folk—were allowed to remain in the country.

The city was ruthlessly destroyed and burnt; the walls were demolished; the soldiers apparently carried out the work of spoliation systematically. They broke up and carried away the two bronze columns, the bronze laver and all the metal furnishings which could be removed from the Temple court. Such was the fate of Jerusalem. The author—or authors—of the Book of Lamentations give a picture in moving terms

[1] Nebuzaradan is a literal transcription of the Babylonian name Nabu-zer-iddin (Nabu gives a sowing). His title is that used by court officials of high rank. In Israel 'Shema' 'servant of Jeroboam' is a well-known title, see *Samaria Capital of the Kingdom of Israel*, p. 76, fig. XX.

[2] Seventy-one, to be precise, if the account given in II Kings 25.18–19, is complete.

[3] According to Jeremiah 52.29, these numbered 832, and a second convoy which followed five years later included 745 Jews (Jer. 52.30). The total number deported amounted to 4,600 persons. This is a much more modest reckoning than that given in the Book of Kings where the first convoy alone is said to have included ten thousand persons (II Kings 24.14). The greater part of the population in fact remained in Judah, and it is necessary to bear this in mind in order to understand the problems which arose at the time of the return from exile.

of this scene of desolation. 'The city sits solitary . . . become as a widow. Her nights are spent in weeping and her tears are on her cheeks. . . . The ways of Sion mourn: no more do pilgrims come to the feast! All her gates are desolate . . . Jerusalem spreads out her hands in supplication. There is none to comfort her. Joy is fled from our heart, our dances are changed to mourning. The crown is fallen from our head. . . .'[1]

*　　　*　　　*

While he was laying siege to Jerusalem, the king of Babylon decided at the same time to take those cities of Judah (fig. XXXVII) which lay on the route to Egypt and thus facilitated the military intervention of Pharaoh. One after another was attacked, the last to fall being Lachish and Azekah.[2] Excavations at Lachish have revealed twenty-one inscribed ostraca (fig. XXXVIII) which clearly date from this period of the city's history.[3] Some of these tablets are letters sent from Hosha'yahu, who commanded a post farther north (possibly Beth Shemesh), to Ya'ush, Governor of Lachish. Most of them were found in a room close to the curtain wall linking the two bastions of the city gate. Ya'ush was commander at

[1] Lam. 1.1–2; 4.17; 5.15–16.

[2] Jer. 34.7. Lachish is now Tell Duweir, Azekah, Tell Zakariya.

[3] These ostraca will be discussed in detail in a forthcoming study. In the present work only those features which are directly relevant to our subject will be mentioned. These documents have given rise to a considerable body of published work which will be listed in full in our later book. The standard studies are: H. Torczyner, *Lachish* I, *The Lachish Letters* (1938); D. Diringer in *Lachish* III, pp. 331–9 (1953).

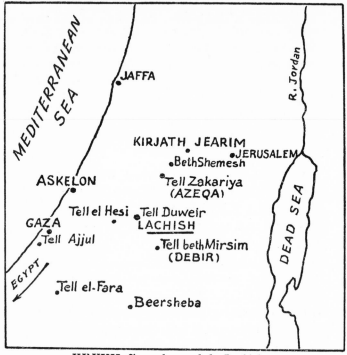

XXXVII. Jerusalem and the Lachish area

Lachish but he also exercised authority over the surrounding district. Letters were therefore sent to him reporting events or asking for instructions.

They are couched in extremely respectful terms. Hosha'yahu, for example (fig. XXXVIII) expresses himself thus:[1]

[1] Letter II. So far as possible the arrangement of the lines and the order of the words have been reproduced here.

To my lord Ya'ush. May Yahweh cause my lord to hear tidings of peace every day! Who is your slave [but] a dog, that my lord has remembered his slave? May Yahweh reveal (?) to . . .[1] a matter which I did not know.'

Letter IV ends thus:

'. . . and he [Ya'ush] would know, concerning the beacons[2] of Lachish, that we are watching, according to the instructions that my lord has given, for we do not see [the signals of] Azekah.

This text is extremely important, for it should be compared with two passages from Jeremiah:[3] 34.7, where Lachish and Azekah are mentioned in connection with Nebuchadrezzar's campaign, and 6.1, where a signal (*mas'et*) is spoken of. As regards the first passage, the Biblical text is placed in its historical setting by a secular document. In the second, a word of doubtful meaning is elucidated and defined.

Ostracon VI is also very informative, if the proposed restorations of the text are correct. This letter, which is also addressed to Ya'ush, reads:

[1] The end of the letter has been the subject of much discussion. H. Michaud, 'Les ostraca de Lakish conservés à Londres', *Syria*, XXXIV (1957), translates it thus: 'May Yahweh show favour to my lord! You say what I did not know!' (or 'what you did not know!').

[2] Signalling by means of fires (or smoke) was a common practice in the ancient world; the earliest evidence is to be found in the Mari letters (eighteenth century B.C.). See G. Dossin, 'Signaux lumineux au pays de Mari', *RA*, XXXV (1938), pp. 174–86.

[3] R. Dussaud, in *Syria*, XVII (1936), p. 388, was one of the first, with F. Albright in *BASOR*, 61 (1936), p. 15, to make this comparison.

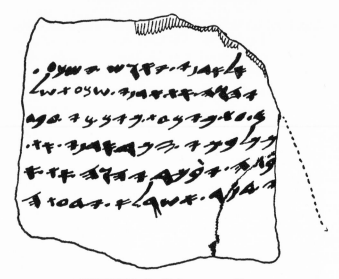

XXXVIII. Lachish ostracon No. 2

'And behold: the words of the [prophet] are not good; they reduce morale,[1] they sap the strength of the country and the city.'[2] This prophet has been identified with Uriah, son of Shemaiah of Kiriath-jearim[3] or with Jeremiah himself.[4] Undoubtedly Jeremiah's preaching would have 'reduced morale'

[1] Literally, 'they weaken the hands', which makes the correspondence with Jer. 38.4 even more striking. See below.

[2] R. Dussaud's translation in *Syria*, XIX (1938), p. 262.

[3] Torczyner, *op. cit.*, p. 66. This prophet is referred to in Jer. 26.20.

[4] Dussaud, *loc. cit.*, p. 263. This identification is supported by H. Michaud in an unpublished thesis 'Les lettres de Lakish et l'Ancien Testament'.

and 'sapped the strength of the country (Judah) and the city (Jerusalem)'. That, in fact, was what his ministers complained of to the king (Zedekiah), saying: 'Let this man [Jeremiah] be put to death, because he weakens the hands of the men of war that remain in this city [Jerusalem], and of all the people, in speaking such words to them.'[1]

Jeremiah did not confine himself to preaching in Jerusalem submission to the Babylonians; he sent messages. One of his letters to the deportees in Babylon has been preserved.[2] Moreover, an ostracon (III) sent by the same Hosha'yahu provides the following information: 'As for the letter which Tobiyahu, the King's servant, took to Shallum, son of Yaddua, *from the prophet*, saying: "Beware!", your slave has sent it to my lord [Ya'ush].'

There were, of course, prophets in Judah, but the mention of *the* prophet suggests that it refers to a prophet of wide reputation who was actively opposed to the generally accepted policy of the time. Moreover, at the date when this letter was written, Uriah who, on this point held the same views as Jeremiah, was dead. Jeremiah was indeed *the* prophet, and it may be assumed that the allusion is to him.[3]

[1] Jer. 38.4. Albright, *The Biblical Period*, p. 46, also draws attention to the similarity of these terms.

[2] Jer. 29.

[3] This identification was suggested by R. Dussaud in *Syria*, XIX (1938), p. 267 and by Jack, H. Michaud, and A. Vincent. It is not accepted by de Vaux (*RB*, 1939, p. 206). Diringer, *op. cit.*, p. 337,

No inference can be drawn from the mention of Mibtahiyahu son of *Yirmiyahu* (ostracon I, 4) since, according to the prophet's own testimony (16.2), Jeremiah was not married. The evidence of ostracon III, 14–18 is doubtful in view of the widely different interpretations which specialists have given to the information it records: according to some, a commander of the army, the son of Elnathan, went down to Egypt to extradite Hodawyahu, son of Ahiyahu, and his men;[1] in the opinion of other scholars, this expedition was only for the purpose of collecting stores;[2] yet others consider that the commander of the army[3] went to assemble an expeditionary force.[4]

Whatever interpretation is adopted, it corresponds to the political situation at the time: Judah and Egypt were allies, and the Judaean troops could easily cross

thinks it too uncertain to make a definite pronouncement. In ostracon XVI, 5 also 'the prophet' is mentioned, but his name is given. Unfortunately, however, only the last syllable *ahu* remains. But Jeremiah was not the only prophet whose name (Jirmiyahu) ended in this way. Torczyner and Ginsberg identify 'the prophet' with Uriah. J. Obermann, '*The Prophet*' *in the Lachish Ostraca*, and W. D. Thomas, '*The Prophet*' *in the Lachish Ostraca*, both adopt a sceptical position.

[1] Dussaud, *loc. cit.*, p. 263. A similar expedition had taken place some years before: Elnathan, son of Achbor, had been sent to Egypt to bring back Uriah who had fled thither (Jer. 26.22–3).

[2] R. de Vaux in *RB*, 1939, pp. 189–90; Albright in *BASOR*, 82 (1941), p. 21.

[3] His name is read in various forms according to the epigraphists: Jikbarijahu, Kabbirijahu, Kabarijahu, Konijahu.

[4] H. Michaud, unpublished thesis. Diringer, *op. cit.*, p. 333, gives the names of those who took part, but does not specify the nature of the expedition on which they were engaged.

the frontier. This is relevant to the information contained in both Biblical and secular texts. It is not necessary to subscribe to the view of Torczyner, who declares of ostracon III that it 'may almost be regarded as an authentic chapter of Holy Scripture';[1] but at the same time the importance of this correspondence for Biblical studies should not be minimized. It is not a matter of chance similarities or mere coincidences. The similarities are repeated so frequently and correspond so exactly with the Biblical narratives that the impression of certainty is difficult to resist. Indubitably no other archaeological discovery has brought the person and the times of Jeremiah so close to us.

But the prophet's troubles were not over. Having destroyed Jerusalem and deported the upper classes of the population,[2] Nebuchadrezzar appointed a Judaean as governor of the province and its remaining inhabitants. This was Gedaliah, son of Ahikam, son of Shaphan.[3] In the course of his excavation of Duweir-Lachish, Starkey discovered the impression of a seal on which was an inscription[4] two lines long that the orientalist S. H. Hooke readily deciphered: 'To Gedaliah who is over the house,'[5] and identified

[1] Torczyner, *op. cit.*, p. 62.
[2] See above, p. 98.
[3] II Kings 25.22; Jer. 40.5.
[4] *ILN*, 10 Aug. 1935, p. 241, fig. 5.
[5] S. H. Hooke in *PEF.QS.*, Oct. 1935, pp. 195–6; Diringer, in *Lachish* III, p. 348.

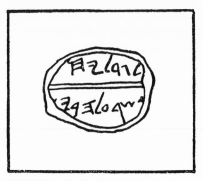

XXXIX. Seal of Gedaliah (from Vincent, Jérusalem de l'Ancien Testament, *II, p. 655)*

this individual as the Governor of Judah. There seems no reason to reject this identification which exactly fits the historical context. Gedaliah belonged to a family of high-ranking officials, 'directors' or 'stewards of the palace', who, for two generations, had held high office at the court of Judah;[1] Shaphan, his grandfather, under Josiah;[2] Ahikam, his father, under Josiah and Jehoiakim.[3] The Lachish seal shows that in Zedekiah's time, Gedaliah had a similar position at the palace in Jerusalem. Both his father Ahikam and his uncle Gemariah had supported and protected Jeremiah,[4] that is to say, they agreed with his

[1] R. de Vaux, 'Le sceau de Godolias, ma'tre du Palais,' *RB*, 1936, pp. 96–102.

[2] II Kings 22.3.

[3] II Kings 22.12; Jer. 36.21–4.

[4] Jer. 26.24; 35.25.

pro-Babylon policy. No doubt Gedaliah had been influenced by them and most probably himself supported a movement which was realistic rather than defeatist. This may explain why Nebuchadrezzar chose him and why Jeremiah, when he was released while already on his way to exile, went back to join Gedaliah and lived near him at Mizpah.[1]

The new Governor set himself to achieve some relaxation in the conditions of life. His watchword was: return to normal ways, which, for the mainly peasant population, meant harvest your grapes, gather your fruits and prepare your oil. The policy was one of appeasement,[2] but it was not acceptable to the nationalist party of which Ishmael was one of the leaders. Although he was aware of their hostility towards him, Gedaliah received a deputation headed by his enemy. While they were at a meal, Gedaliah with his officers was assassinated.[3] Two days later the same fate overtook some pilgrims who were on their way to Jerusalem. Their bodies were thrown into a well.[4] One of Ishmael's associates was called Jaaza-

[1] Jer. 40.1–6.

[2] It was the policy advocated by Jeremiah some years earlier when he wrote to the deported population: 'Build ye houses, and dwell in them; and plant gardens, and eat the fruit of them.' (29.5).

[3] Jer. 40.7–41.3.

[4] Jer. 41.4–9. W. F. Badé, who excavated Mizpah (the present-day Tell en-Nasbeh) thought that this well could be identified with one he had discovered in 1926 (*Tell en-Nasbeh*, I, p. 217). But the authors of this report, published after Badé's death, rejected this interpretation which had already been disputed by Father Vincent, *RB*, 1927, p. 418.

XL. Seal of Jaazaniah (ibid., *p. 657*)

niah;[1] a seal belonging to him was found at Mizpah
(fig. XL) in an unopened tomb.[2] It is inscribed with
the words, 'To Jaazaniah, slave of the king', and a
drawing of a cock.[3]

After the murder of Gedaliah, Ishmael, fearing re-
prisals at the hands of the Babylonians, fled and took
refuge with the Ammonites beyond Jordan. Those
who had survived the massacre left Judah, against
the advice of Jeremiah, whom they had consulted,

[1] II Kings 25.24; Jer. 40.8.

[2] W. F. Badé, 'The Seal of Jaazaniah', *ZAW*, LI (1933), pp. 150–6;
C. C. McCown, *Tell en-Nasbeh*, I, p. 163.

[3] This bird is very seldom found on seals before the eighth century. There is one on a very fine Assyrian cylinder found at Nimrud,
see *Iraq*, XII (1950), p. 170; XVII (1955), pp. 97–8 and Plate XI, 1.

and went into Egypt taking the prophet with them.

The whole company came to Tahpanhes[1] and settled there. These Jews, cut off from the Temple, now began to practise the cult of the 'Queen of Heaven', a goddess whom they were not ashamed to associate with Yahweh. Jeremiah threatened these renegades with destruction by the sword or by famine, but his words aroused no response. And on this note of failure ends the story of one of the greatest of the prophets—the man of Anathoth.[2]

*   *   *

What, in the meantime, was happening to the exiles, in particular those who had been deported with the first convoy in 597? Once again unexpected information has been provided by archaeological researches. As already mentioned[3] Nebuchadrezzar had deported King Jehoiachin, with his mother, his wives, members of his household and army officers[4] together with a considerable number of skilled craftsmen. Mattaniah-Zedekiah had become king in Jerusalem, but his reign lasted only till 586, the date of the destruction of the city and his own capture.[5] The Biblical record has nothing to say about what happened in Palestine and in Babylon after the assassination of Gedaliah, at least during the reign of Nebuchadrezzar, which lasted till 562.

---

[1] Now Tell Defenneh, west of the Suez Canal.   [2] Jer. 1.1.
[3] See above, p. 90.
[4] II Kings 24.10–17; II Chron. 36.10.
[5] See above, p. 91.

But fortunately this gap may be filled, thanks to the Babylonian archives. Among the cuneiform tablets recovered in Babylon by Koldewey, E. F. Weidner found some on which the name of the captive king of Judah, Jehoiachin, was written. This was a notable discovery, the significance of which was universally recognized.[1] The tablets can be dated from the tenth to the thirty-fifth year of Nebuchadrezzar's reign, that is between 595/594 and 570/569 B.C. The name of Jehoiachin appears on four of them in connexion with the distribution of foodstuffs, more particularly oil and sesame. It is spelt in two different ways: Ja'ukînu or Jakûkînu, and he is described as 'king of the land of Jâhudu'.[2] His five sons[3] are mentioned as being with him, but their names are not given,[4] and

[1] E. F. Weidner, 'Jojachin, König von Juda, in babylonischen Keilschrifttexten', in *Mélanges syriens*, II, pp. 923–35. A great number of orientalists and exegetes have made use of this documentation and discussed it, for example, de Liagre Böhl, 'Nebukadnezar en Jojachin' in *Opera minora*, pp. 423–9; W. F. Albright, 'King Joiachin in Exile', *BA*, V, pp. 49–55.

[2] Sometimes written Jaudu or Jakudu. On one tablet Jakûkînu is called '*son* of the king of Jakudu'; as Weidner suggests, this may be an error on the part of the scribe.

[3] Weidner considers that it would have been difficult for the king, who was taken into exile at the age of eighteen (II Kings 24.8), to be already the father of five sons only five years later; the tablet in fact dates from the thirteenth year of Nebuchadrezzar, that is 592 B.C. Weidner suggests that 'brothers' should be understood, not sons. Albright, *op. cit.*, p. 52, prefers the Babylonian data. It may, however, be doubted whether the word 'sons' should be taken in its strict sense. The Mari tablets provide numerous examples of people being designated 'sons' of the king when they were not really his sons.

[4] Their names are given in I Chron. 3.17, where, however, Jeconiah is said to have seven sons.

in one document there is a reference to 'eight men of
the land of Jahudu'. It is noteworthy that, though his
companions received a very limited ration, the king
himself was lavishly supplied.[1] This may be an indication of the high regard in which the king was held,
or, on the other hand, it may suggest that from his
allocation the king was expected to provide for the
needs of a great number of dependants. The latter
seems more probable.

Thus the tablets provide confirmation of the captivity of the king and his family. The fact that these
documents were found in the north-eastern angle of
the Southern Citadel, an area which Koldewey identified as the site of the 'hanging gardens',[2] does not
prove that the prisoners were lodged there.[3] In
palaces that have been pillaged in the past—which
has happened here—objects have often been moved
and abandoned at random.[4] Even if they were found
in their original place, these tablets would have been
kept in a library of archives rather than in a prison.
They are orders for deliveries 'at the hands of
Qanâma'[5] to those for whom they were intended.

Jehoiachin and his companions were well treated,

---

[1] Two half *sila* for the five sons of the king (almost two pints), four
sila (five pints) for the eight men, but ten *sila* for the king.

[2] See above, pp. 40–2.

[3] Weidner, *loc. cit.*, p. 927.

[4] For example, the royal archives at Mari were scattered through
the rooms of the palace when the city fell.

[5] This note, which occurs on two tablets, may be thus understood.

as is evident from the fact that in these official documents the exiled king is referred to by his title. This prerogative has been confirmed by archaeological evidence. Excavations at Beth Mirsim and Beth Shemesh uncovered three impressions of a seal (fig. XLI) inscribed with the words: 'To Eliakim steward

XLI. Seal of Eliakim (from AASOR, *XII, p. 78)*

of Jaukin'.[1] Jaukin may certainly be identified with Jehoiachin.[2] Thus it is clear that the captive king retained his estates in Judah, no doubt crown property, administered by a steward. The occupation of the throne by Zedekiah was not accepted by the party which may be called 'legitimist', and which some of

[1] W. F. Albright, 'The Seal of Eliakim and the latest pre-exilic History of Judah, with some observations on Ezekiel', *JBL*, LI (1932), pp. 77–106; *BA*, V (1942), pp. 50–1; *AASOR*, XXI–XXII (1943), pp. 66, note 9. Drawing of the seal, *ibid*, Plate 29, 9.

[2] This was suggested by Father Vincent at the first inspection. A photograph of the impression on a jar is given in *AASOR*, XII, Plate 40, 5.

11. *Palm plantation at Babylon*

12. *By the rivers of Babylon*

13. *Babylon Halt*

the prophets supported. So Hananiah proclaimed to the people as the word of Yahweh that Jeconias[1] (that is, the exiled king) would return to Palestine with his companions. The tablets which Weidner published preserve the names of some of these: Ur-milki, Gadi-ilu, Shalamjâma[2] the gardener, Samaku-jâma.[3] But the prisoners from Judah were inter-mingled with other peoples from the various con-quered territories: Philistines (two sons of the king of Ashkelon), Phoenicians (people of Tyre, Byblos and Arvad), Elamites, Medes, Persians, Ionians, Lydians, Egyptians.[4] A hotch-potch of peoples and races col-lected, by the will of a conqueror, in the very place where, according to the Biblical tradition, Yahweh first ordained the dispersion of mankind (Gen. 11.9).

In 562 Nebuchadrezzar died after reigning for forty-three years. Its long duration[5] accounts for the success which marked his rule, both within and be-yond the frontiers of his own country. The territory controlled by Babylon was roughly identical with the area known to-day as the Near East. The whole of western Asia from Susa to the Mediterranean, from the upper Tigris (excluding Nineveh) to the shores

[1] The Greek form of Coniah (Jer. 22.28) or Jeconiah (I Chron. 3.16) another name for Jehoiachin. For Hananiah's prophecy see Jer. 28.1–4.

[2] Cf. Shelemaiah, a name which appears on the Lachish ostraca.

[3] Cf. Semachiah on the Lachish ostraca and also in I Chron. 26.7.

[4] For details see Weidner, *loc. cit.*, pp. 928–35.

[5] It lasted as long as the reign of Hammurabi.

of the Persian Gulf, from Taurus to the 'cataract of Egypt' lay in the power of one man. The capital had been restored to its former glory, and not only Babylon itself but all the great cities of southern Mesopotamia, raised again from their ruins, bore witness to the power and the genius of one of the most adventurous builders of the ancient world. It was, nevertheless, in the face of this striking achievement, that the voices of the prophets resounded, prophesying doom: 'Babylon shall be destroyed. In her place shall be a desolation, a dry land and a desert'.[1] The time had not yet come for this destiny to be fulfilled, but with the death of Nebuchadrezzar, Babylon's decline began.

* * *

Within five years, three kings followed him: Awêl-Marduk, Nergal-shar-usur, Labashi-Marduk. The first, called Evil-Merodach in the Old Testament,[2] began his reign by pardoning Jehoiachin, king of Judah. He released him from prison and treated him honourably,[3] but kept him at Babylon close to himself. This 'freedom under supervision' lasted until the

[1] Jer. 50-1. For a discussion of the authenticity of this passage see *Bible du Centenaire*, II, p. 579, note *c*.

[2] II Kings 25.27 (Marduk is foolish) a corruption of Awêl-Marduk (the man of Marduk).

[3] Giving him the clothing of a free man and access to the royal table. The expression 'to eat at the table' of an important personage indicated a sign of great favour. It frequently occurs in the Bible (II Sam. 9.7, 13; I Kings 2.7; 18.19; Matt. 8.11; 9.10; Luke 7.37; John 12.2, etc.), but it was in use much earlier, for example in the Mari archives (eighteenth century B.C.)

king's death,[1] the date of which is not known.[2] It
may have occurred during the reign of Nabonidus,
the last of the Babylonian kings, who occupied the
throne for seventeen years but witnessed the downfall
of his country.[3]

Now began one of the most troubled periods in
Babylonian history, of which echoes may be found in
the book of Daniel. The central figure is the enig-
matic Nabonidus,[4] who led the conspiracy which
overthrew the young king Labashi-Marduk, and himself seized the throne in 556 B.C. He was the son of a
priest, Nabû-balât-su-iqbi, and a high-priestess of the
cult of the god Sin at Haran, and inherited from his
parents a strong leaning towards religious practices.
This is the explanation of his passion for restoring

---

[1] II Kings 25.27–30; Jer. 52.31–4.

[2] Jehoiachin was taken prisoner at the age of eighteen and was
liberated after thirty-seven years in captivity; he would therefore be
fifty-five years old.

[3] If Jehoiachin had been alive in 539 at the coming of the Persians
they would certainly have restored him to his throne when they
allowed the Jews to return to Palestine, and this would have solved
some of the problems raised by the 'Return'. The only surviving
member of the royal family was a son of Jehoiachin, the mysterious
Sheshbazzar, 'prince of Judah' (Ezra 1.8; 5.14–15), whose name is a
typical Babylonian one (Sin-abal-uṣur—may Sin protect the son!).
On this point see *Bible du Centenaire*, III, p. 371, note *b*.

[4] R. P. Dougherty, *Nabonidus and Belshazzar*; Dhorme, 'La mère
de Nabonide' in *RED*, pp. 325–50; 'Cyrus le Grand', *ibid.*, pp.
367–73; 'La fille de Nabonide', in *RA*, XXII (1925), pp. 71–83;
Böhl, 'Die Tochter des Königs Nabonid', in *Opera Minora*, pp. 174–
87; S. Smith, *Isaiah Chapters XL–LV*, pp. 24–48, and bibliography,
p. 115.

temples, seeking the foundation offerings deposited by his predecessors but also adding his own.[1]

Moreover he was a visionary and attached great importance to dreams, which seem to have brought him to the verge of madness. Religious practices may often become sacrilegious practices, as when the king gathered together in Babylon the statues of the gods who had 'presided over the great days of Chaldean glory'.[2] He became even more unpopular when he suspended the celebration of the traditional New Year festival in Babylon until the shrine of Sin at Haran had been rebuilt.[3] From the seventh year of his reign (548 B.C.), however, he was forced to hand over his

[1] For example the cylinders which he deposited at each of the angles of the ziggurat at Ur and which Taylor discovered in 1854, or the tablet which he caused to be buried in the foundations of the temple of Shamash at Sippar, and on which he inscribed the name of one of his illustrious predecessors, Naram-Sin, king of Accad, whom he places 3,200 years before his own time, that is about 3,750 B.C. The scribe, or the king, was about 1,500 years out!

[2] Dhorme, 'Cyrus le Grand', in *RED*, p. 368.

[3] Nabonidus indicates that fifty-four years had elapsed from the destruction of the temple of Haran by the Medes until it was restored by him. If this information is correct it fixes the date of the return of the moon god to his temple: 610–54=556, that is the year of the king's accession to the throne of Babylon. For the cult of Sin at Haran, see Dhorme's works cited above and J. Lewy, 'The late Assyro-Babylonian cult of the Moon and its culmination at the time of Nabonidus,' in *HUCA*, XIX (1945–8), pp. 405–89. Dhorme refuted these conclusions with some vigour in *RED*, pp. 330–8. According to Sidney Smith, *op. cit.*, p. 34, the temple of Sin at Haran was entirely restored in 553.

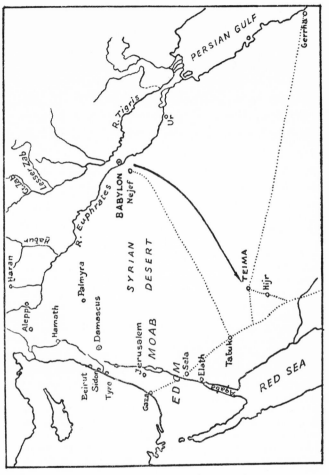

XLII. Babylon and the Arabian desert

authority to his eldest son, Bêl-shar-uṣur,[1] and to live in retirement at Teima[2] (fig. XLII), as an exile or for reasons of state.[3] In his absence, and for several years, the New Year festival could not be held in Babylon.[4] Nabu did not come from Borsippa nor did Marduk emerge from Esagila. A time of national mourning lasted till the king's return[5] in the seventeenth year of his reign, 539 B.C. Then the festivals were celebrated once more, but almost too late, for the land

[1] Undoubtedly the King Belshazzar of Dan. 5.1. See H. H. Rowley, 'The historicity of the fifth chapter of Daniel', in *Journal of Theological Studies*, XXXII, pp. 29 *et seq.*

[2] This was certainly the present oasis of Teima in north Arabia. Dhorme was doubtful for some time (as in *RED*, pp. 368, 370) but finally accepted this identification (*RB*, 1925, p. 466, *RED*, p. 163 and the correction on p. 334, note 3). It is supported by S. Smith, *op. cit.*, pp. 37 and 136.

[3] According to Sidney Smith, his stay in the town which followed his campaign against it was dictated by political considerations. From there Nabonidus could command the caravan traffic between the Red Sea and the Persian Gulf (S. Smith, *op. cit.*, pp. 38-40). It may be objected, however, that the king could have deputed this task to one of his officers. Concerning the time spent by Nabonidus in Teima, see R. Dussaud, 'Sur le chemin de Suse et de Babylone', in *Mélanges Franz Cumont*, pp. 143-50. Another result of his stay there was the introduction of the cult of Sin into Teima, where a temple of Sin was discovered, dated by Canon Ryckmans to the sixth century B.C. The caravan traffic through Teima is mentioned in Job 6.19; Isa. 21.14. See also Gen. 25.15, where Teima is referred to as a son of Ishmael.

[4] One of a number of indications that Belshazzar was only a regent and did not exercise royal powers. For the New Year ceremonies see S. Pallis, *The Babylonian Akîtu festival.*

[5] For these events see S. Smith, *Babylonian historical texts relating to the capture and downfall of Babylon.* It is not possible to date with any certainty Nabonidus' return to Babylon; it might have been in the fourteenth year.

had been invaded by the armies of Cyrus the Great.

This is not the place to describe in detail the successive conquests[1] by which, after defeating the Median king Astyages (*c.* 553),[2] Cyrus the Persian, son of Cambyses, became the most formidable figure in the ancient Near East. Having conquered the Lydian kingdom of Croesus, Cyrus turned on Babylon, the only power able to stand in the way of his road to empire. But there was no longer any reason to fear resistance; gone were the days of Nebuchadrezzar; Babylon was the statue with feet of clay described in the book of Daniel.[3] The king had seen in a dream a statue made of various metals: the head of gold, the breast and arms of silver, the belly and thighs of bronze, the legs and parts of the feet of iron.[4] A stone hewn from a mountain smote the feet of the

[1] Dhorme, 'Cyrus le Grand', *RED*, pp. 351–82, from which our information is mainly drawn.

[2] S. Smith, *op. cit.*, p. 35, prefers 550–49 B.C.

[3] All exegetes agree that the Nebuchadrezzar of Dan. 2.1; 3.1; 4.1, is in fact Nabonidus. Cf. A. Lods, *Histoire de la littérature hébraïque et juive*, pp. 837–8; W. Baumgartner, 'Ein Vierteljahrhundert Danielforschung', in *Theologische Rundschau*, XI (1939), pp. 59–83, 125–44, 201–28. See also Dhorme, in *RED*, p. 369, note 1.

[4] Dan. 2.31–3. Statues of mixed materials were common in ancient times. There are some of gold and ivory (chryselephantine); of bronze overlaid with gold or silver (statuettes found at Byblos, Ras Shamra and Larsa); of wood with bronze plating, such as the lions in the temple of Dagan at Mari; of bronze and stone, as the baal of Ras Shamra; of bitumen plated with copper (at Tell el-Obeid). A ceremonial axe found at Ras Shamra is made of copper, iron and gold. This list is, of course, not exhaustive.

statue (which were made of clay and iron;[1] they were shattered into fragments and the statue collapsed.

No more apt description could be found of that empire, whose façade was so magnificent, but whose foundations were so unstable and insecure[2] that it fell at the first assault. Cyrus himself led the attack. Two days after taking Sippar, which Nabonidus had evacuated, the Persian army encamped below the walls of Babylon (16 Teshri [September to October] 539). The town fell, probably owing to treason, while the Babylonians were feasting.[3] Two Babylonian deserters,[4] Gobryas and Gadatas, had precipitated the disaster. They entered Babylon and hurried to the palace, but Nabonidus was not there, having again gone in flight. He was overtaken on the way to Borsippa and made prisoner[5] but was released by

[1] No doubt this means that the core was of baked earth overlaid with iron. There is no known example of this.

[2] A just comment is expressed in Dan. 2.43: 'iron doth not mingle with clay.'

[3] Xenophon and Herodotus remarked on the disorder which prevailed in Babylon. No doubt this tradition underlies the account of Belshazzar's feast in Dan. 5. The headlong nature of the collapse is clearly indicated in Isa. 47.11.

[4] Schwenzer, 'Gobryas', in *Klio*, 18, pp. 41–58; 226–52; Dhorme in *RED*, p. 372. S. Smith, *op. cit.*, pp. 44, 47 distinguishes between Ugbaru-Gobryas, Governor of Gutium who captured Babylon, and Gubaru, a Persian official appointed Governor of Babylon by Cyrus. It was the former who contributed to Cyrus' victory.

[5] According to S. Smith, *op. cit.*, p. 44, Nabonidus did not come to Babylon after the fall of Sippar but attempted to escape in a south-westerly direction towards the desert. Finding the road blocked by Arabs, he returned to Babylon which, in the meantime, had fallen

Cyrus. His son Belshazzar was, however, put to death.[1]

It is not easy to understand the harsh treatment meted out to him by contrast with the clemency extended to his father,[2] for Cyrus entered Babylon not as a conqueror but as a liberator. The temples were not profaned and the safety of the city was guaranteed. Cyrus took as his title 'King of Babylon, Sumer and Accad, and the four countries of the world'. He went further and claimed to have been chosen by Marduk as is shown in a Babylonian text: 'Marduk gave thought to all the lands, he saw them and sought a righteous king, a king after his own heart whom he would lead by the hand. He called his name Cyrus, king of Ashan! and appointed him to be king over all things'.[3] For the prophet Isaiah, Cyrus, the

into the hands of the Persians, and was there taken prisoner. A different interpretation given by Dhorme in *RED*, pp. 372–3 is adopted here.

[1] According to Dan. 5.30, the execution took place at night, and this corresponds with the accounts given by classical authors. But if this statement is accurate the one which follows is not: 'Darius the Mede received the Kingdom, being about sixty-two years old' (5.31). For historically, there is no room for Darius the Mede, son of Xerxes, between Belshazzar and Cyrus. Cf. H. H. Rowley, *Darius the Mede*, p. 9; 'The Unity of the Book of Daniel', in *HUCA*, XXIII, p. 263.

[2] According to Berossus, Nabonidus died in exile in Carmania, one of the distant eastern provinces of the Achaemenian kingdom. On the other hand, Xenophon states that the king was killed (*Cyropaedia*, VII, v, 30).

[3] Dhorme, *La religion assyro-babylonienne*, p. 157; also 'Cyrus le Grand' in *RED*, p. 375, where he notes the striking comparison with Isa. 45.4: 'I have called thee by thy name: I have surnamed thee, though thou hast not known me'; where Yahweh addresses Cyrus. Cf. also *Bible du Centenaire*, II, p. 398, note *a*.

chosen one of Marduk, was Yahweh's anointed: 'Thus says Yahweh to his anointed, to Cyrus whom he has taken by the right hand, to subdue the nations be-fore him . . . I will give you the treasures of darkness and the wealth hidden in secret places'[1] (45.1, 3). Cyrus thus seemed to be the man appointed to cap-ture the defeated cities, but also to redress the wrongs of the humiliated gods. In Babylonia he returned to their own cities the gods which Nabonidus had car-ried away to his capital.[2] As far as Palestine was con-cerned, he was commanded by Yahweh to rebuild Jerusalem and restore the Temple.[3] Here, of course, there was no divine effigy to be returned to its place, but the gold and silver vessels of the cult, which Nebuchadrezzar had removed, were given back.[4] Finally, those who had been deported were given per-mission to return to their own country and this was forthwith announced in an edict promulgated in 538 B.C.[5] The reception given to this act of liberation must now be considered.

✻   ✻   ✻

[1] The wealth of Croesus, king of Lydia, who was conquered in 547 (see p. 119 above), treasures hoarded in Babylon (Jer. 50.37; 51.13).　　　　[2] Dhorme, 'Cyrus le Grand', in *RED*, p. 376.

[3] Ezra 1.1–4; 6.3–5. Cf. Isa. 44.28; Yahweh says of Cyrus: 'He is my shepherd, and shall perform all my pleasure: even saying of Jerusalem, She shall be rebuilt; and of the Temple, Thy foundation shall be laid.'　　　[4] Ezra 6. 5.

[5] On the edict of Cyrus see R. de Vaux, 'Les décrets de Cyrus et de Darius sur la reconstruction du Temple,' in *RB*, 1937, pp. 29–57. This article includes an extract from the cylinder discovered at Babylon by Rassam, beginning with the words, 'Cyrus—chosen by Marduk.'

It has already been mentioned that Jeremiah ad-
vised the exiles to settle down in the land to which
they had been deported, to build houses and plant
trees (Jer. 29), in other words, to organize themselves
for a long period of captivity; he even announced that
it would last seventy years.[1] But he had no doubt
whatever that Babylon, though it was the instrument
of Yahweh's wrath against Judah, would in its turn
be struck down, and this was why no resistance must
be offered. Babylon would eventually succumb to the
violence of the destroyers sent by Yahweh, as the sea
covers everything and carries everything away.[2]

The exiles had found asylum not only in the city
itself[3] but throughout the neighbouring country and
especially in Nippur, in southern Mesopotamia.[4]

---

[1] Jer. 29.10. The exile did not last so long; including the first
deportation the period was fifty-nine years. Whitley in *Vetus Testamentum*, IV, 1954, pp. 60–72, suggests that the Jews, after the exile,
counted seventy years, from 586 to 516, the date of the completion of
the second Temple.

[2] Jer. 50–1. It must be recognized that the question of the authenticity of these two chapters raises many problems which are sum-
marized in the *Bible du Centenaire*, II, p. 579. The present author,
however, regards them as the work of Jeremiah. The prophet thought
that Babylon would fall at the hands of the Medes (51.11, 27–8).
Thus the oracle must have been uttered before the rise of the Persian
hegemony, and certainly before 550. If the authorship of Jeremiah is
admitted, there is no reason to doubt the date (fourth year of Zedekiah, or 593 B.C., according to Jer. 51.59).

[3] The cuneiform tablets already referred to (p. 110) provide evidence for this, at all events as regards the more notable prisoners.

[4] The present-day Nuffar, the excavation of which was begun in
1889 and, after a long interval, was resumed in 1948 and is now
being carried on by an American expedition.

Ezekiel's 'river Chebar' (1.3) may be identified with the *naru kabaru*, which, in cuneiform texts, designates a tributary of the Euphrates that waters the city where Enlil, god of the earth, was specially venerated. It is obvious that the words in Psalm 137—'By the rivers of Babylon'—must be taken in the widest sense. These rivers are the canals which irrigated the country rather than the Euphrates itself. In the ancient world, all rulers regarded as one of their primary responsibilities the construction and maintenance of the canals[1] by which the water so vitally necessary for cultivation was carried deep into the interior, miles from the river's course.

Many of the villages where the deported population was settled are known by name, though their sites cannot be identified: Tel-Melah, Telharsha, Cherub, Addan, Immer (Ezra 2.59), Casiphia (Ezra 8.15); Tel-Abib.[2] It is clear, however, that the country was incomparably more fertile than Palestine, and that, after the planting, the only labour required was to supervise the irrigation system.

It would, therefore, be inaccurate to represent the life of the exiles as completely without activity, nor is this suggested by the cry of the psalmist. The Jews were seated 'by the rivers, their harps[3] hanging from

[1] See, for example, the correspondence of king Hammurabi of Babylon and king Zimri-Lim of Mari.

[2] Ezek. 3.15. The Jews gave the Hebrew name Tel-Abib (mound of ears of corn) to the Babylonian Tel-Abubi (mound of the flood).

[3] An instrument with ten strings, according to Josephus.

the branches of the willow trees[1] (Plate 12), weeping
and remembering Sion and refusing to sing (fig.
XLIII) a song of Sion' in that strange land.[2] But this

XLIII. *Prisoners singing (from Gadd,* The Stones of
Assyria, *Pl. 20, p. 176)*

must have been a sabbath, when the Jews, observing
the rest required by their religion, were gathered to-

[1] The Hebrew word *'arábîm* is sometimes translated 'poplars', but
these trees are not found in central or southern Mesopotamia,
whereas willows grow in profusion on the banks of the canals.

[2] An Assyrian relief from the palace of Sennacherib at Nineveh
shows a group of prisoners under escort singing to the accompaniment
of a harp(?). See C. J. Gadd, *The Stones of Assyria*, Plate 20, p. 176
(BM 124947).

gether on the banks of the canals.[1] The songs they refused to sing were religious hymns which they considered it sacrilege to sing on foreign, that is, unclean, soil.[2]

So far as their material existence was concerned, the exiles quickly adapted themselves to the liberal treatment they received, and their settlements became prosperous.[3] This is clear from the fact that, when the edict authorizing the exiles to return to Jerusalem was published by Cyrus, a considerable number of them elected to remain in Babylon, reluctant to forfeit their comfort and imperil their fortunes for the sake of an uncertain future. About fifty thousand went back to Palestine.[4] This figure, however, raises serious difficulties.[5] The others continued to work and get rich. Ezra alone must have taken to Jerusalem more than £30,000 in gold and silver.[6] At

---

[1] Such places constituted the earliest synagogues, but at a much later date they were still used. In the time of St Paul, the Jews of Philippi met together on the bank of a river (Acts 16.13). See also Ezra 8.21.

[2] The same idea is expressed in Hosea 9.3–15 and Amos 7.17.

[3] A. Lods, *Les prophètes d'Israël et les debuts du judaïsme*, pp. 201–3.

[4] Ezra 2.64–5 (42,360 + 7,327 + 200 = 49,877).

[5] A. Lods, *op. cit.*, pp. 216–17, considers that 'it is not wise to rely on this list'.

[6] Ezra 8.26–7. This journey, as van Hoonacker suggests, probably should be dated 397 B.C. For a general account of this problem of chronology see H. H. Rowley, 'The chronological order of Ezra and Nehemiah,' in *Memorial Ignace Goldziher*, pp. 117–49; 'Nehemiah's Mission and its background,' in *BJRL*, March 1955, pp. 528–61. A complete bibliography on the subject is to be found in these two essays.

the time of Artaxerxes I (465–424 B.C.) and Darius II
(424–405 B.C.) there is evidence that at Nippur a
trading firm, Murashu and Son, was carrying on
buiness on a very large scale, operating as a bank,
an agricultural agency and a trading organization.[1]
Its head office was at Nippur, but its branch estab-
lishments and its sixty odd agencies formed a net-
work covering some two hundred local centres and
extending from north of Babylon to the 'Land of the
Sea'. Moreover among the clients of the bank may
be found an unusual number of Jewish names—
among them the name of Yahweh in the forms Yahu,
Yamah or Ya—which indicates the size of the Jewish
population in Babylon more than a hundred years
after the edict of Cyrus. These records—some 730
tablets have been noted[2]—make it possible to 'reconstruct the day-to-day activities of one of the oldest
banks in the world' and reveal the social and juridical
organization of a feudal agricultural society in which
the Jews were no longer in the position of a deported
population. They were, in fact, completely absorbed
and it is understandable that they had no desire to

[1] The most recent study on this subject is that of Guillaume Car-
dascia, *Les Archives des Murašû, une famille d'hommes d'affaires babyloniens
à l'époque perse* (455–403 B.C.); a summary of this work by J. Nougayrol,
'Une des plus anciennes banques du monde: la maison Murasu à
Nippur', was published in the *Journal des Savants*, 1952, pp. 85–8.
There is a bibliography in Cardascia, *op. cit.*, pp. ii–iii. See also
O. Eissfeldt in *ZAW*, 1935, pp. 60 *et seq.*

[2] The earliest document dates from 455, the latest from 403 B.C.
Cardascia, *op. cit.*, p. 1.

uproot themselves and exchange the familiar situation in Babylon for the uncertainties of Palestine.

The exiles did not consist only of business men; certain individuals among them exercised what was in fact a spiritual ministry. 'Priests and prophets' (Jer. 29.1, 15) had also been deported, and some of them (Ahab, Zedekiah,[1] Shemaiah[2]) regarded it as their mission to incite their countrymen to resistance and to encourage them in false hopes. It seems that the king of Babylon severely repressed their intrigues.

Ezekiel took his stand against these false prophets. As already mentioned (p. 91), he had been deported with the first convoy in 597, before the fall of Jerusalem, probably at the age of twenty-five. Thus if he was still alive at the time of the edict of Cyrus, he would have been eighty-four. Since there is no mention of his return to Palestine, it may be supposed that he died in Babylonia and was buried there, near the body of his wife, 'the delight of his eyes[3]'.

Ezekiel, more than any other prophet, was a child of his age and his environment; his utterances cannot be understood apart from the events which occasioned them. He proclaimed first the inevitable destruction of Jerusalem, but also the divine chastisement which was to fall on the Ammonites, the Moabites, the Edomites, and the Philistines—the nearest neighbours of Judah.[4] But neither the Phoeni-

---

[1] Jer. 29.21. [2] Jer. 29.24, 31.
[3] Ezek. 24.16. [4] Ezek. 25.

cians[1] nor the Egyptians (Ezek. 29–32) were to escape. King Nebuchadrezzar could not fail to approve of such an attitude, which seemed to discourage political ambitions, but it is clear that the conduct of the prophets cannot be judged by such obvious considerations; for them Yahweh was making use of these foreign rulers to effect his own purposes.

With the fall of Jerusalem in 586 the character of the prophetic utterances changes abruptly: Ezekiel's theme is now return and restoration. But, paradoxical as it might appear, all this was in fact to take place, though how, and by what means was not made clear. Those who had a sense of the realities of the situation would certainly recognize in the prophet's words the fall of Babylon, for the disappearance of Edom (Ezek. 25) could have only local repercussions and the invasion of the barbarian hordes from the north would be crushed by Yahweh himself (Ezek. 38–9). Here also Ezekiel could prophesy without fear, since he was not implicating the existing power. In the thought and the actions of Ezekiel there are obvious signs of the 'influence of the art, the myths and the customs of Babylonia, the place where he was living;'[2] and this is abundantly illustrated and emphasized by the discoveries of archaeologists. It is clear, for

[1] Ezek. 26–8, which gives the most vivid picture ever painted by an historian of antiquity of the Phoenician culture and its two capital cities Tyre and Sidon.

[2] A. Lods, *op. cit.*, p. 258; A. Jeremias, *Das Alte Testament im Lichte des Alten Orients*, pp. 698–710.

example, that there are undeniable Babylonian
elements in the vision of the chariot of God with
which the collection of oracles opens,[1] even though

XLIV. Person with two faces (two-faced god)

the total impression conveyed by Ezekiel defies pictorial representation. Each of the four winged beings
of his vision has a fourfold face, displaying the features
of a man, a lion, a bull, and an eagle. There are, in

[1] Ezek. 1.5–28; G. R. Driver, 'Ezekiel's Inaugural Vision', in
Vetus Testamentum, I, pp. 60–2.

XLV. Person with four faces (from Frankfort,
More Sculpture from the Diyala Region,
Pl. 77)

Mesopotamian iconography, examples of two-faced[1]
(fig. XLIV) and four-faced[2] (fig. XLV) figures, but
the faces are always identical. On the other hand, in
Assyrian works may be found: the body of a man with
the head of an eagle or of a lion; a lion's body with a

---

[1] The two-faced god of the cylinders, prototype of the Roman
Janus.
[2] H. Frankfort, 'More Sculpture from the Diyala Region' (*OIP*,
LX), Plates 77, 78.

man's head; a bull's body with a man's head.[1] All these elements are associated in the winged bulls represented as guarding the entrance to the royal

XLVI. Assyrian bulls from the palace at Khorsabad (Archéologie mésopotamienne, *I, fig. 18*)

palace (fig. XLVI); here may be seen a man's head, eagles' wings, the breast of a lion and the body of a bull. These are precisely the elements of the prophetic vision which must have been inspired, consciously or

[1] This is the androcephalous bull of the Sumerian epoch. For examples of small statuettes of this type, see the author's *Tello,* Plate XII.

unconsciously, by the reliefs which, in the sixth century, were still to be seen, even though the Assyrian towns, Khorsabad, Nineveh and Calah, lay in ruins.[1] The significance of these hybrid figures has long been, and will probably continue to be, a subject of discussion, but the greatest mystery is why Christian iconography should have retained, as symbols of the four evangelists, the man, the bull, the eagle, and the lion, which are to be seen on the tympana of romanesque churches but which, long before Ezekiel and the Apocalypse,[2] had belonged to Mesopotamian mythology, for two thousand years before the Assyrians, the Sumerians had used them.[3] In the vision of Ezekiel, these creatures upheld a chariot which was also a throne (Ezek. 1.15). Thus the conception, current in Israel, of Yahweh enthroned between or above the cherubim reappears.[4] In this connexion reference is often made to Hittite monuments in which two winged sphinxes placed side by side form the base of

[1] Nineveh had fallen in 612 B.C. and Ezekiel was deported in 597 B.C. This would suggest that the deported population did not travel by way of the middle Euphrates, but crossed upper Gezira and reached the upper Tigris. It is necessary to correct Auvray's reference in *Ezéchiel*, p. 22, note *a*, to 'enormous statues [which] gúarded the palace at Babylon, three specimens of which now adorn the Assyrian gallery of the Louvre'. No statue of this character ever existed at Babylon, at all events none has been found there. Those in the Louvre came from Khorsabad.

[2] Rev. 4.7.

[3] See the author's study 'Glyptique de Mari et mythologie orientale', in *Studia Mariana*, pp. 119–23. The androcephalous winged bull will be discussed in *Le Musée du Louvre et la Bible*.

[4] II Kings 19.15; I Chron. 13.6; Ps. 80.1; 99.1; Isa. 37.16.

a circular pedestal[1] which rests upon their backs, or again to reliefs in which two lions are introduced.[2]

But these examples are not well chosen, for in each case what rests on the base is a column, not a god. On the other hand a statue at Carchemish represents a bearded god seated, or rather enthroned, on a block flanked by two grinning lions[3] controlled by a man with the head of a bird of prey (fig. XLVII).

The prophet's vision concludes with a description which may well be quoted in full: 'Above the firmament which extended over their heads was the likeness of a sapphire stone in the form of a throne; and on this form of a throne was to be seen *as it were the form of a man on high. And again I saw as it were polished amber, like fire, shining all round about, within which was that man; from the appearance of his loins upward and from the appearance of his loins downward, I saw as it were fire and a bright light shining around him. Like the appearance of the bow which is in the cloud on a day of rain, so was the appearance of that light shining around him.'[4]

There is an Assyrian document which illustrates this passage; it is a picture in enamel from the palace of Tukulti-Ninurta II (890–884) which was discovered by Andrae at Ashur.[5] There are human figures whose

---

[1] That of Zendjirli of the eighth century B.C., in Bossert, *Altanatolien*, p. 900.

[2] At Tell Tainat, of the ninth century B.C., *ibid.*, 873.

[3] *Ibid.*, 830.

[4] Ezek. 1.26–7.

[5] W. Andrae, *Farbige Keramik*, Plate 8.

XLVII. Statue from Carchemish (from Bossert, Altanatolien, 830)

heads alone (fig. XLVIII) are visible and above them
the blue firmament in which there is the 'form of a
man' extended on a circle of fire and holding a bow.
Ezekiel ends his vision with the words: 'This was the
likeness of the glory of Yahweh' (Ezek. 1.28); if
the word Ashur were substituted for Yahweh the

XLVIII. Ashur in the flaming wheel (from Gressmann, AOBAT,
333)

prophet's description could be applied to the Ashur
monument.[1]

There is yet another indication of foreign influence
in the passage where the prophet, describing the plan
of the Temple, sees a cherub with two faces, one of a
man and the other of a lion.[2] Although the position
of the faces is not the same, there is an undeniable

[1] Gressman, *AOBAT*, p. 95, had drawn attention to this similarity,
but referred only to Ezek. 1.26.

[2] Ezek. 41.18–19.

resemblance to a carved tile from Carchemish (fig.
XLIX) on which a winged beast is represented in

IL. Tile from Carchemish (from Bossert, Altanatolien, *852)*

profile with two heads, one of a lion and one human.[1]
At one point the prophet is ordered to take a brick

[1] Bossert, *op. cit.*, 852, a ninth-century relief. A drawing of this
beast, brought into conformity with the text of Ezekiel, may be
found in Vincent, *Jérusalem de l'ancien Testament*, II, p. 482, fig. 151.

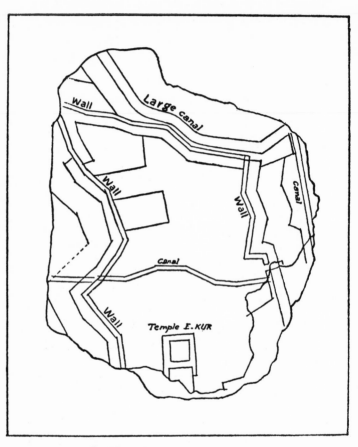

L. Plan of a city found at Nippur

and draw on it the plan of a town, Jerusalem (Ezek. 4.1). This is specifically a Babylonian characteristic; plans of districts, houses, and also of cities were often incised on clay tablets. One of these (fig. L), found at Nippur, has in fact a sketch of the city[1] showing the important monuments, the canals and the walls, and

LI. Besieged city. Shalmaneser's campaign (from King, Bronze reliefs from the Gates of Shalmaneser, *Pl. L)*

it was possible to check the accuracy of the plan by the findings of archaeological research. The prophet's sketch, moreover, was to represent the city in a state of siege, encircled by trenches and camps and assaulted by battering rams (Ezek. 4.2). Striking illustrations of this are provided by Assyrian monuments on which are represented besieged fortresses (fig. LI)

[1] H. V. Hilprecht, *Explorations in Bible Lands*, p. 518; there is a better reproduction in S. N. Kramer, *From the Tablets of Sumer*, fig. 80.

undergoing assault and breached by means of siege engines manipulated by engineers.[1]

Yahweh had said: 'I have set Jerusalem in the midst of nations and countries are round about her' (Ezek. 5.3). An exactly similar conception may be seen on a tablet in the British Museum[2] on which a city is represented as the centre of the world.[3]

Sword, famine, and pestilence were the weapons with which Yahweh was to chastise the house of Israel.[4] It may be recalled that in the epic of Gilgamesh, Ea rebukes Enlil for not having used lion, wolf, famine, and pestilence to punish men instead of destroying them by the flood.[5] Such exact similarities cannot be due merely to chance.

In his vision of the idolatrous cults that were being practised at Jerusalem, Ezekiel saw 'all kinds of forms of creeping things and four-footed beasts and abomin-

[1] There are numerous examples on the Balawat bronze plaques (ninth century B.C.) and the ornamental reliefs in the palaces at Khorsabad, Nineveh and Nimrud (ninth-seventh centuries B.C.).

[2] BM, 92687. A map of the world in Babylonian times, cf. Unger, *Babylon*, Plate 3.3; Jeremias, *Handbuch der Altorientalischen Geisteskultur*, pp. 148, 151, fig. 89–90. See also fig. I, p. 16 above.

[3] The 'navel of the world' may still be seen to-day in the Greek choir of the Church of the Holy Sepulchre in Jerusalem. In medieval maps the countries of the world were placed around Jerusalem as their centre, an obvious derivation from the text of Ezekiel.

[4] Ezek. 6.11; 7.15; 12.16. In other passages a fourth affliction is added—wild beasts (5.17; 14.15–19).

[5] See *The Flood and Noah's Ark*, p. 30 and p. 31, note 1. The epic dates from the seventh century B.C.

able beasts . . . portrayed upon the wall round about.'[1]
One is reminded, of course, of the animals worshipped
by the Egyptians,[2] but it should not be forgotten
that in Babylon the prophet would have seen not
only bulls but also the dragons of Marduk, and com-
posite[3] and 'abominable' beasts, adorning the Ishtar
gate.[4] Moreover, the women 'weeping for Tammuz'
(Ezek. 8.14) were mourning for a god of Babylonian
origin,[5] Dumuzi, who had been included in the
Phoenician pantheon under the name of Adonis and
whose death was commemorated every year. We are
told (Ezek. 8.16) that twenty men officiated in the
cult of the sun.[6] The number twenty is associated
with Shamash, the Babylonian sun god. It is said also
that the votaries of the cult 'put the branch to their
nose'.[7] It is highly probable that this is a reference to
the gesture which the Assyrians called *labân appi* and
which is represented on numerous monuments.[8] It
is a ritual gesture of humility and abasement before
the majesty of the god.

[1] Ezek. 8.10 The authenticity of the text has been disputed, see
Bible du Centenaire, II, p. 608.

[2] This point is made by A. Lods in the *Bible du Centenaire*.

[3] Among which were to be found the features of serpents, lions,
dragons, birds of prey and scorpions. Jeremias has drawn attention
to this connexion in *Das Alte Testament . . .*, p. 704.

[4] See above, pp. 30, 31.   [5] A. Moortgat, *Tammuz.*

[6] The massoretic text has 25, but the figure 20 given in the Septuagint seems preferable.

[7] A difficult and disputed passage (Ezek. 8.17).

[8] For example, the stele of Esarhaddon at Sendjirli, and the
Naqi'a bronze in the Louvre (see fig. XXXI, p. 78 above.)

When Yahweh proclaimed that the idolatrous inhabitants of Jerusalem would be slain, it is understood that those who had not transgressed would escape death. The six men appointed to carry out the slaughter were to spare all those whose foreheads had been marked with a cross by a scribe who was entrusted with the duty of selecting them. We are told that he had a writer's inkhorn at his side (Ezek. 9.2). The figure of a scribe is frequently represented on Assyrian reliefs, particularly in the act of counting war loot or severed heads.[1] He holds a stylus in one hand and in the other a tablet or writing-board. In 1953 Mallowan found a number of these objects when excavating Nimrud.[2] They were made of ivory and of wood[3] and contained a slab of wax for writing on. The group of seven men—the six executioners and the scribe—recall the seven Babylonian demons[4] shown on exorcism tablets[5] (fig. LII).

[1] See the Sennacherib relief in the British Museum (BM 124955) in *Iraq*, XVII (1955) Plate III, 2; see also *Nineveh and the Old Testament*, p. 67, fig. XV.

[2] See *Iraq*, XVI (1954), pp. 98–107.

[3] D. J. Wiseman, 'Assyrian Writing-Boards', in *Iraq*, XVII (1955), pp. 3–13; Margaret Howard, 'Technical Description of the Ivory Writing-Boards from Nimrud,' *ibid.*, pp. 14–20. Even if these tablets (there were 16 of them) were really leaves of a book, each of them may be regarded as a model of a writing-board.

[4] Thureau-Dangin, 'Rituel et amulettes contre Labartu', in *RA*, XVIII (1921), pp. 161–98.

[5] The best example of these is one in the Clercq collection, *Catalogue* II, Plate XXXIV. It is intact and thus makes it possible to reconstruct other specimens in the same series which exist only in fragments.

LII. Seven Babylonian demons (from RA, *XVII (1921), Pl. 1)*

The fate of King Zedekiah is compared to that of a lion fallen into a pit and taken alive and dragged, by hooks through his nose, into a cage.[1] All this recalls the customary hunting techniques[2] and also the harsh treatment meted out to prisoners of war, for which there is both literary[3] and pictorial[4] evidence.

Consulting the omens was an official state institution throughout Mesopotamia. Inspection of the liver (hepatoscopy) was one of the methods used for divining the future. According to Ezekiel (21.21) this was practised by the king of Babylon. Diviners were pro-

[1] Ezek. 19.4, 9.

[2] This is how lions were caught for the king of Mari, Zimri-Lim.

[3] Sargon of Accad kept Lugalzaggisi, the conquered king of Uruk, in a cage. Identical cages, used for the same purpose, were placed at the east gate of Nineveh.

[4] Sargon of Assyria and Esarhaddon kept prisoners on a leash with hooks through their jaws (a relief from Khorsabad and steles from Zendjirli and Tell Ahmar).

[143]

vided with clay or bronze models of livers, the different malformations of which indicated events which were to come (fig. LIII).[1]

In another oracle, Ezekiel introduces two women,

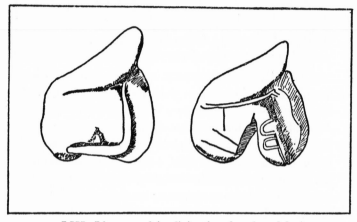

LIII. Livers used in divination found at Mari

Oholah and Oholibah. The latter, who personifies Jerusalem, 'doted upon the Assyrians, governors and commanders, clothed most gorgeously, horsemen riding upon horses, all young and desirable' (Ezek. 23.12). She displays the same liking for the 'Chaldeans', when she saw 'on the wall their images por-

[1] The author found thirty-two models of livers in the palace of Mari, evidently used for this sort of divination. This is the largest collection that has ever been found. Cf. M. Rutten, in *RA*, XXXV (1938), pp. 36–52.

trayed in vermilion'.[1] Obviously there is a reference here both to the tiles ornamented with reliefs in colour and to the paintings which decorated the walls of the great Assyrian palaces at Khorsabad, Nimrud and Tell Ahmar.

We have cited only those elements in the oracles of the prophet in which Mesopotamian influence can be illustrated from iconography and confirmed by archaeology. Our last two examples relate to Ezekiel's vision of the new Jerusalem and the Temple. The prophet, carried away in spirit to the land of Israel, saw a man whose bodily appearance was like bronze, holding in his hands 'a line of flax and a measuring reed' (Ezek. 40.3). Now these two objects—a line and a measuring reed (fig. LIV)—occur very frequently on Mesopotamian monuments[2] and they are generally recognized as instruments used for marking out the ground-plan for buildings in course of construction.[3]

[1] Ezek. 23.14. One of the styles of painting found at Tell Ahmar is of this character: the outlines of the figures were sketched in red, the contours being emphasized in black. Thureau-Dangin, *Til-Barsib*, p. 48, 62. The same technique is to be seen in the Kassite paintings of Dur-Kurigalzu, *Iraq*, VIII (1946), p. 81.

[2] Stele of Ur-Nammu found at Ur, on which the moon god Nannar has them in his hands when he receives the homage of the king who has come to get instructions concerning the ziggurat he is about to build.

[3] Some orientalists favour a different interpretation and regard these objects as symbols of power because they are seen in the hands of gods. Cf. E. D. van Buren, 'The Rod and the Ring', in *Archiv Orientalni*, XVI (1950), pp. 434–50.

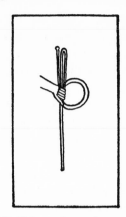

LIV. 'Measuring rod' and line

This revelation of supernatural architecture—the building of the Temple in the new Jerusalem—is conveyed to Ezekiel by that mysterious 'man' who cannot be other than an angel.[1] Inevitably one is reminded of the vision in which Gudea, the Sumerian prince of Lagash, saw 'a man whose stature was equal to the heaven, whose stature was equal to the earth and the crown on his head was that of a god', a man whom he did not recognize and who 'commanded him to build him a house (=temple)'.[2] Other deities

[1] *Bible du Centenaire*, II, p. 683, note *h*.

[2] Gudea, *Cylinder A*, IV, 14–20, translated by Fr. Thureau-Dangin, *Inscriptions de Sumer et d'Akkad*, p. 141. In the translation by M. Lambert and R. Tournay in *RB*, 1948, p. 410, there are some modifications, but these have no bearing on the figure of the god Ningirsu, tutelary deity of the city.

(Nisaba, Nindub) also appeared and marked out the plan. Thus the building was completed only after several divine beings had approved it. The Temple of Ezekiel's vision, which in fact was never built,[1] was, in the same way not the work of a human architect but the design of Yahweh, the Holy God, communicated through the mysterious man,[2] the attentive guide and the interpreter of the divine purposes.

[1] See *The Temple of Jerusalem*, pp. 61–7.
[2] He is present throughout the vision only withdrawing when Yahweh himself speaks (cf. Ezek. 43.6 *et seq.*).

EPILOGUE

The Achaemenian conquest finally destroyed the independence of Babylon. In the exhilaration of his victory Cyrus assumed the title of 'King of Babylon' as well as 'King of the lands'. His successors until Xerxes continued to use it, but thereafter abandoned it. The title was not revived either by the Greeks or the Parthians who followed them, for its significance had diminished with the passing of the years. The city, however, continued to be inhabited, in spite of the foundation of a new capital, Seleucia, on the Tigris. But the appearance on the scene of the Parthians (124 B.C.) accelerated the decline and stripped the city of her substance. The last mention of Babylon occurs on a tablet dating from 10 B.C. Her monuments had perished. Now the words of the prophets were literally fulfilled:

'And Babylon, the glory of kingdoms,
The splendour and pride of the Chaldeans,
Will be like Sodom and Gomorrah, when God himself
    overthrew them.
It will never more be inhabited,
It will remain unpeopled till the end of time.
No Arab will pitch his tent there, nor will any shepherd fold his flocks.
But wild beasts will shelter there,

Owls will fill its houses.
Ostriches will dwell there
And satyrs will dance.
Dogs will howl in its castles
And jackals in its pleasant palaces.' (Isa. 13.19–22.)

'She shall be inhabited no more for ever
   or peopled to the end of time.'   (Jer. 50.39.)

'Everyone who passes by Babylon shall be appalled and
   shall hiss because of all the blows which she has
   suffered.
She shall be wholly desolate.'   (Jer. 50.13.)

The fulfilment was complete: solitude and mounds
of ruins. As a final irony, the Baghdad to Bassorah
railway was laid only a few feet away from the hill
'Babil'. A wooden placard bears an inscription in
English and Arabic: 'Babylon Halt. Trains stop here
to pick up passengers' (Plate 13). Not even a station,
merely a halt! After stopping to pick up passengers—
often there are none—the train goes on again and
only its whistling breaks the silence.

CHRONOLOGICAL
AND SYNOPTIC TABLES

I. FROM THE FOUNDING OF BABYLON TO THE CAPTURE OF SAMARIA

BABYLONIA	ASSYRIA	EGYPT	PALESTINE	REFERENCES
Dynasty of Accad (25th–23rd cent.)	Tudia	IVth dynasty Pyramids of Ghizeh		
IIIrd dynasty of Ur (22nd–21st cent.)	Ushpia			
		Middle Kingdom (2160–1580)		
1st dynasty of Babylon (1894–1595)				
Hammurabi (1792–1750)	Shamshi-Adad (1823–1791)		Patriarchal migration	Gen. 11.31–2
			Abraham arrives in Palestine	Gen. 12.5
Hittite raid on Babylon (c. 1595)		New Kingdom (1580–1090)		

Babylon	Assyria	Egypt	Israel / Palestine	Bible
The Kassites in Babylon (beginning of 16th cent.)				
			The Exodus. Moses	Ex. 12.37-41
Melishippak II (12th cent.)	Tukulti-Ninurta I takes Babylon (1243–1207)	XXth dynasty (1200–1085)	The Israelites in Palestine	Joshua
Elamite raid End of Kassite dynasty (1171)			The Judges David (c. 1000) Solomon (963–923)	Judges II Sam. 2 I Kings 2
Eriba-Marduk (802–763)	Tiglathpileser III (745–727)	XXIVth dynasty (730–715)	Jeroboam II (786–746) Capture of Samaria by the Assyrians (721)	II Kings 15-23 II Kings 17
Marduk-apal-iddin III (722–711)			Hezekiah (716–687) ISAIAH	II Kings 18 (Merodach-bala-dan)

II. From the Capture of Samaria to the Neo-Babylonian Period

ISRAEL	JUDAH	ASSYRIA	BABYLONIA	EGYPT	REFERENCES
Capture of Samaria (721)	Hezekiah (716–687)	Sargon II (721–705)	Marduk-apal-iddin (721–711)	XXIVth dynasty (730–715)	II Kings 20. 12–13; Isa. 39.1
Samaria colonized	Micah	Sennacherib (704–681)			II Kings 18. 13–19, 37. II Chron. 33
	Manasseh (687–642)	Esarhaddon (681–669)		Tirhakah (689–683)	II Kings 19.37 II Chron. 33
	Amon (642–640)	Ashurbanipal (668–631)	Shamash-shum-ukin (668–648)	Psammetichus (663–609)	II Kings 21. 19–26. II Chron. 33. 21–25

[154]

Josiah (640–609) Josiah's reform (622) JEREMIAH ZEPHANIAH NAHUM	Ashur-etil-ilani (631–628)	Kandalanu (647–627)		II Kings 22–23 II Chron. 34
	Sin-shumu-lishir (627) Sin-shar-ishkun (627–612)			
Josiah killed at Megiddo (609)	Fall of Nineveh (612)	Nabopolassar (626–605)	Necho (609–594) Necho slays Josiah at Megiddo	II Kings 23.29
Jehoahaz (609)	Ashur-uballit (611–606)			II Kings 23.30 II Chron. 33. 1–4
	Capture of Haran (609)			

III. From the Neo-Babylonian Period to the Return from Exile

JUDAH	BABYLONIA	EGYPT	PERSIA	REFERENCES
{ Eliakim { Jehoiakim (609–598)	Nabopolassar (626–605) Battle of Carche- mish (605)	Necho (609–594)		II Chron. 36.5–8 Jer. 46.2 II Kings 24.1–5
HABAKKUK	Nebuchadrezzar (605–562)			
JEREMIAH				II Kings 24.8–9 II Chron. 36.9 Babylonian Tab- lets
{ Jehoiachin { Jeconiah (598) Capture of Jeru- salem (597)	First deportation (597) EZEKIEL	Apries (588–568)		II Kings 24.10–16; II Chron. 36.10; Ezek. 1.2; II Kings 24.17
{ Mattaniah { Zedekiah (597–586)	Zedekiah sends an embassy to Baby- lon			Jer. 29.3

Judah	Babylon	Egypt	Persia	Scripture
2nd capture of Jerusalem (586)	Second deportation (586)	Amasis (568–526)	Cyrus (558–529)	II Kings 25.1–21; Jer. 52; Ezek. 24; Lachish Ostraca; II Kings 25.23–26; Jer. 41; II Kings 25.27–30; Jer. 52:31–34
Assassination of Gedaliah	Awêl-Marduk (561–560)			Isa. 45.1,3; Jer. 50–51; Daniel
	Nergal-shar-usur (559–556)			
	Labashi-Marduk (556)			
	Nabonidus (556–539)			
	Bêl-shar-usur (Belshazzar)			Dan. 5.1
	Fall of Babylon (539–8)		Cyrus takes Babylon (539–8) Edict of Cyrus	
Return from Exile 1st company (537) Zerubbabel Joshua				Ezra 1–2; Ezra 3.2

SELECT BIBLIOGRAPHY

The bibliography given below is limited to essential books and important articles having a direct bearing on our subject.

Excavations

Andrae, W., *Babylon. Die versunkene Weltstadt und ihr Ausgräber Robert Koldewey*, 1952.

Jordan, J., *Guide through the Ruins of Babylon and Borsippa*, 1937.

Koldewey, R., 'Die Pflastersteine von Aiburschabu in Babylon', *WVDOG*, 2, 1901.

'Die Tempel von Babylon und Borsippa', *WVDOG*, 15, 1911.

'Das Ischtar-Tor in Babylon', *WVDOG*, 32, 1918.

Das wiedererstehende Babylon, fourth edition, 1925.

(*The Excavations at Babylon*, 1914).

Koldewey, R., and Delitzsch, F., 'Die hettitische Inschrift der Königsburg', *WVDOG*, 1, 1900.

Koldewey, R., and Wetzel, F., 'Die Königsburgen von Babylon. I. Die Südburg. II. Die Hauptburg und der Sommerpalast Nebukadnezars in Hügel Babil', *WVDOG*, 54, 55, 1931, 1932.

Oppert, J., Reports of the scientific expedition in Mesopotamia carried out by order of the Government from 1851 to 1854 by Fulgence Fresnel, Felix Thomas and Jules Oppert. Vol. I. *Relation du voyage et résultat de l'expédition*, 1863; Vol. II. *Déchiffrement des inscriptions cunéiformes*, 1859; *Atlas*, with text by Oppert and drawings by Thomas.

Reuther, O., 'Merkes. Die Innenstadt von Babylon', *WVDOG*, 47, 1926.

Weissbach, F., 'Babylonische Miscellen', *WVDOG*, 4, 1904.

Wetzel, F., 'Die Stadtmauern von Babylon', *WVDOG*, 48, 1930.

Wetzel, F., and Weissbach, F., 'Das Hauptheiligtum des Marduk in Babylon, Esagila und Etemenanki', *WVDOG*, 59, 1938.

Monographs on Babylon

King, L. W., *A History of Babylon*, 1915.

Unger, E., *Babylon. Die heilige Stadt nach der Beschreibung der Babylonier*, 1931.

  'Babylon', *RLA*, pp. 330–69.

Weissbach, F., 'Das Stadtbild von Babylon', *AO*, 5, 4, 1904.

  'Babylonien', *RLA*, 1931, pp. 369–84.

Winckler, H., 'Geschichte der Stadt Babylon', *AO*, 6, 1, 1904.

Critical studies and exegesis of Biblical texts

Auvray, P., *Ezéchiel*, 1947.

Auvray, P., and Steinmann, J., *Isaïe*, 1951.

Bentzen, A., 'Daniel' (*Handbuch zum A.T.*, O. Eissfeldt), second edition, 1952.

Bertholet, A., *Hesekiel*, 1936.

Condamin, A., *Le livre de Jérémie*, 1936.

Select Bibliography

Dhorme, E., in *La Bible*. I. *L'Ancien Testament*, Bibliothèque de la Pléiade, 1956. The most recent translation with a verse by verse commentary.

Eissfeldt, O., *Einleitung in das Alte Testament*, 1934.

Fohrer, G., and Galling, K., *Ezéchiel*, I, 1955.

Ginsberg, H., *Studies in Daniel*, 1948.

Humbert, P., *Problèmes du livre d'Habacuc*, 1944.

Lods, A., in *Bible du Centenaire*, 1947. (An indispensable authority, on account of the accuracy of the translation and the abundant notes.)

North, C. R., *Isaiah 40–55*, 1952.

Rudolph, W., 'Jeremia' (*Handbuch zum A.T.*, O. Eissfeldt), 1947.

Vaux, R. de, *Les Livres des Rois*, 1949.

Zimmerli, W., *Ezechiel, 1–2*, 1955.

Babylonian monuments and texts

A. MONUMENTS:

Gressmann, H., *Altorientalische Bilder zum Alten Testament*, 1927.

Grollenberg, L. H., *Atlas of the Bible*, 1956.

Pritchard, J. B., *The Ancient Near East in Pictures relating to the Old Testament*, 1954.

Wright, G. E., *Biblical Archaeology*, 1957.

Wright, G. E., and Filson, F. V., *The Westminster Historical Atlas to the Bible*. Revised edition, 1957.

B. COLLECTIONS OF TEXTS:

Gressmann, H., *Altorientalische Texte zum Alten Testament*, 1926.

Pritchard, J. B., *Ancient Near Eastern Texts relating to the Old Testament*, 1955.

Select Bibliography

Manuals and general works

Galling, Kurt, *Biblisches Reallexikon,* 1937.
    Textbuch zur Geschichte Israels, 1950.
Jeremias, A., *Handbuch der altorientalischen Geisteskultur,* second edition, 1929.
    Das Alte Testament im Lichte des Alten Orients, fourth edition, 1930.
Lods, A., *Les prophètes d'Israël et les débuts du judaïsme,* 1935.
    La religion d'Israël, 1939.
    Histoire de la littérature hébraïque et juive, 1950.
Noth, M., *Die Welt des Alten Testaments,* second edition, 1953.
    Histoire d'Israël, 1954.
Pallis, S. A., *The Antiquity of Iraq,* 1956.
Olmstead, A. T., *History of the Persian Empire,* 1948.
Ricciotti, G., *Histoire d'Israël,* I, II, 1947–8.
Vincent, P. L. H., *Jérusalem de l'Ancien Testament,* II, III, 1956.

Articles and studies

Albright, W. F., 'The Seal of Eliakim and the latest pre-exilic History of Judah, with some observations on Ezekiel', *JBL,* LI, 1932, pp. 77–106.
    'A Supplement to Jeremiah: the Lachish Ostraca', *BASOR,* 61, 1936, pp. 10–16.
    'The oldest Hebrew Letters: the Lachish Ostraca', *BASOR,* 70, 1938, pp. 11–17.
    'A Re-examination of the Lachish Letters', *BASOR,* 73, 1939, pp. 16–21.
    'The Lachish Letters after five years', *BASOR,* 82, 1941, pp. 18–24.

[161]

Select Bibliography

'King Joiachin in Exile', *BA*, V, 1942, pp. 49–55.

'The Biblical Period': extract from *The Jews: Their History, Culture and Religion*, 1949.

'The Nebuchadnezzar and Neriglissar Chronicles', *BASOR*, 143, 1956, pp. 28–33.

Bade, W. F., 'The Seal of Jaazaniah', *ZAW*, LI, 1933, pp. 150–6.

Baumgartner, W., 'Ein Vierteljahrhundert Danielforschung', *Theologische Rundschau*, XI, 1939, pp. 39–83, 125–44, 201–28.

'Herodots babylonische und assyrische Nachrichten', *Archiv Orientalni*, XVIII, 1, 2, 1950, pp. 69–106.

Bickermann, E. J., 'The Edict of Cyrus in Ezra I', *JBL*, LXV, 1946, pp. 249–75.

Böhl, de Liagre, 'Die Fünfzig Namen des Marduk', *Opera minora*, 1953, pp. 282–312.

'Nebukadnezar en Jojachin', *ibid.*, pp. 423-9.

'Babylon, de Heilige Stad', *ibid.*, pp. 430–62.

'De Chaldeeuwse Dynastie', *Mélanges Byvanek*, 1954, pp. 31–53.

Busink, Th. A., *De Babylonische Tempeltoren*, 1949.

Cardascia, G., *Les Archives des Murašû, une famille d'hommes d'affaires babyloniens à l'époque perse* (445–403 B.C.), 1951.

Dhorme, E., 'La mère de Nabonide', *RED*, 1951, pp. 325–50.

'Cyrus le Grand', *ibid.*, pp. 367–73.

Dougherty, R. P., *Nabonidus and Belshazzar. A study of the closing events of the Neo-Babylonian Empire*, 1929.

Dussaud, R., 'Le prophète Jérémie dans les Lettres de Lachish', *Syria*, XIX, 1938, pp. 256–71.

'Sur le chemin de Suse et de Babylone', *Mélanges Franz Cumont*, 1936, pp. 143–50.

[162]

Select Bibliography

Falkner, Margarete, 'Neue Inschriften aus der Zeit Sin-sharru-ishkun', *AfO*, XVI, 1953, pp. 305–10.

Gadd, C. J., *The Fall of Nineveh*, 1923.

Galling, K., 'Von Nabonid zu Darius. Studien zur chaldäischen und persischen Geschichte', *ZDPV*, 70, pp. 4–32.

Genouillac, H. de, 'Nabonide', *RA*, XXII, 1925, pp. 71–83.

Goetze, A., 'Additions to Parker and Dubberstein's Chronology', *JNES*, III, 1944, pp. 43–6.

Goossens, G., 'Les recherches historiques à l'époque néo-babylonienne', *RA*, XLII, 1948, pp. 149–59.

Gordon, C. H., 'Notes on the Lachish Letters', *BASOR*, 70, 1938, pp. 17–18.

Hooke, S. H., *Babylonian and Assyrian Religion*, 1953.

King, L. W., *Chronicles concerning early Babylonian Kings*, 1907.

Lewy, J., 'The late Assyro-Babylonian cult of the Moon and its culmination at the time of Nabonidus', *HUCA*, XIX, 1945–8, pp. 405–89.

Michaud, H., 'Les lettres de Lakish et l'Ancien Testament'. Unpublished thesis, 1941.

   'L'action politique du prophète Jérémie'. Unpublished thesis, 1946.

   'Les ostraca de Lakish conservés à Londres', *Syria*, 1957.

Obermann, J., '*The Prophet*' in the Lachish Ostraca.

Olmstead, A. J., 'The Chaldaean Dynasty', *HUCA*, II, 1925, pp. 29–55.

Pallis, S. A., *The Babylonian Akîtu Festival*, 1926.

   'The History of Babylon 538–93 B.C.', *Studia orientalia J. Pedersen dicata*, 1953, pp. 275–94.

[163]

Select Bibliography

Parker, R. A., and Dubberstein, W. H., *Babylonian Chronology 626* B.C.–A.D. *45*, 1942.

Ravn, O. E., *Herodotus' Description of Babylon*, 1942.

Rowley, H. H., *Darius the Mede and the four World Empires in the Book of Daniel*, 1935.

'The historicity of the fifth chapter of Daniel', *Journal of Theological Studies*, XXXII, p. 29 f.

'The chronological order of Ezra and Nehemiah', *Memorial Ignace Goldziher*, 1948, pp. 117–49.

'The unity of the Book of Daniel', *HUCA*, XXIII, 1950–1, pp. 233–73.

The Book of Ezekiel in Modern Study, 1953.

Rothstein, J. W. *Die Genealogie des Königs Jojachin und seiner Nachkommen (I Chron. 3.17–24) in Geschichtlicher Beleuchtung*, 1902.

Sidersky, D., 'Contribution à l'étude de la chronologie néobabylonienne', *RA*, XXX, 1933, pp. 57–70.

Smith, Sidney, *Babylonian historical texts relating to the capture and downfall of Babylon*, 1924.

Isaiah Chapters XL–LV. Literary criticism and History, 1944.

Steinmann, J., *Le prophète Ezéchiel et les débuts de l'exil*, 1953.

Thiele, E. R., 'New evidence on the chronology of the last Kings of Judah', *BASOR*, 143, 1956, pp. 22–7.

Thomas, W. D., '*The Prophet*' in the Lachish Ostraca.

Torczyner, H., *Lachish I, The Lachish Letters*, 1938.

Vaux, R. de, 'Le sceau de Godolias maître du Palais', *RB*, 1936, pp. 96–102.

'Les décrets de Cyrus et de Darius sur la reconstruction du Temple', *RB*, 1937, pp. 29–57.

'Les ostraka de Lachis', *RB*, 1939, pp. 181–206.

Weidner, E. F., 'Jojachin, König von Juda in babylonischen Keilschrifttexten', *Mélanges syriens*, II, 1938, pp. 933–5.

'Hochverrat gegen Nebukadnezar II', *AfO*, XVII, 1954–5, pp. 1–9.

Wetzel, F., 'Babylon zur Zeit Herodots', *ZA*, 48, 1944, pp. 45–68.

Assur und Babylon, 1949.

Wiseman, D. J., *Chronicles of Chaldaean Kings (625–556 B.C.) in the British Museum*, 1956.

KEY TO ABBREVIATIONS

AfO: Archiv für Orientforschung.
AO: Der Ale Orient.
AOBAT: GRESSMAN, Altorientalische Bilder zum Alten Testament.
BA: The Biblical Archaeologist.
BASOR: Bulletin of the American Schools of Oriental Research.
BJRL: Bulletin of the John Rylands Library.
HUCA: Hebrew Union College Annual.
ILN: Illustrated London News.
JBL: Journal of Biblical Literature.
JNES: Journal of Near Eastern Studies.
OIP: Oriental Institute Publications.
PEF. QS: Palestine Exploration Fund. Quarterly Statement.
RA: Revue d'assyriologie et d'archéologie orientale.
RB: Revue biblique.
RED: Recueil Edouard Dhorme.
RLA: Reallexikon der Assyriologie.
WEB: KOLDEWEY, Das Wiedererstehende Babylon.
WVDOG: Wissenschaftliche Veröffentlichung der Deutschen Orient-
           Gesellschaft.
ZA: Zeitschrift für Assyriologie.
ZAW: Zeitschrift für die Altestamentliche Wissenschaft.
ZDPV: Zeitschrift des Deutschen Palästina-Vereins.